# ADVANCE PRAISE FOR *CRITICAL RELIEF*

"Dr. Mc Ginley's book offers a refreshing and thought-provoking perspective on the relationship between healthcare administrators (like me) and physicians. While the needs of physicians and the financial goals of hospitals may sometimes seem at odds, this book highlights the importance of understanding and aligning these needs for the greater good of patient care. As a seasoned healthcare administrator, I sometimes find myself torn between advocating for my physicians and ensuring the financial health of the hospital, often feeling it's difficult to do both at once. Dr. Mc Ginley's insightful experience and thoughtful suggestions offer me a new lens through which to view my role, a new perspective from which to approach conversations, and new possibilities for positive outcomes."

**BONNIE MCDONALD** DIRECTOR, VAIL HEALTH CLINICS

"The crisis in US medicine is real. Mark has applied more than 30 years of experience in clinical care and physician leadership to characterize critical elements of the challenges that face us all, physicians and administrators, and has detailed solutions we should be implementing without delay. I cannot recommend this book highly enough!"

**JAMES ORFORD, MBCHB, MPH** INTERVENTIONAL CARDIOLOGIST, INTERMOUNTAIN HEART INSTITUTE

"As a chief medical officer, healthcare consultant, and clinical informatician, I've encountered numerous challenges in driving change within the hospital setting—challenges that often revolve around improving physician relations and fostering collaboration between medical professionals and administrators.

In this context, *Critical Relief* by Dr. Mark Mc Ginley is an invaluable resource and a well-crafted guide for effecting meaningful change. Dr. Mc Ginley deftly combines his extensive experience in critical care with actionable insights into managing relationships among physicians and between physician leaders and administrators. The strategies in this book are both practical and grounded in real-world experience, making them immediately applicable in a variety of healthcare settings. Dr. Mc Ginley's book is extremely timely and deeply researched, informed by the latest developments in healthcare, and it reflects a profound understanding of the current challenges and opportunities facing medical professionals today. This depth of research adds tremendous value to the book, making it not only relevant but also essential reading for those in healthcare leadership."

**DAVID M. MARTORANO, MD** PSYCHIATRIST, AUTHOR OF *IMMORTALITY*, CHIEF MEDICAL OFFICER, WYOMING BEHAVIORAL INSTITUTE

"Dr. Mc Ginley's *Critical Relief: A CEO's Guide to Transforming Hospital Culture* is an insightful guide for healthcare managers. It underscores the importance of acknowledging and engaging with the physician to enhance patient care. Amidst the current crisis of physician burnout and the struggle to retain skilled physicians within the healthcare system, Dr. Mc Ginley's insights are both timely and essential. He advocates for prioritizing physicians as the organization's primary customers, a crucial step for the future of healthcare."

**JANET SCOTT, MBCHB, DIP HIV MAN (SOUTH AFRICA)**
CLINICAL HEAD, D.P. MARAIS HOSPITAL, CAPE TOWN

"This book captures the true thoughts and insights of a practicing physician, which can transform how CEOs and healthcare executives approach their responsibilities in regard to developing physician relationships and commitment to the organization."

**DAVID MECKSTROTH, DHA, MBA, FHFMA**
FORMER CEO, UPPER VALLEY MEDICAL SYSTEM

"Dr. Mark Mc Ginley's book is a transformative guide for any healthcare leader aiming to foster a culture of excellence and compassion. His in-depth insights into leadership and modern physician challenges are both practical and inspiring, making this book an essential read for those committed to elevating hospital culture, physician job satisfaction, health system productivity, and patient care."

**MIKE GORENCHTEIN, MD** GERIATRIC MEDICINE,
LENOX HILL HOSPITAL, NORTHWELL HEALTH

"Dr. Mc Ginley's book *Critical Relief* provides an insider's analysis of the many challenges faced by physicians in today's healthcare environment and describes workable strategies that hospital administrators can employ to optimize the quality of care in their organizations."

**CHARLES J. VAN HOOK, MD** PULMONARY AND
CRITICAL CARE PHYSICIAN

"A must-read for hospital CEOs. Dr. Mc Ginley proposes a low-cost, high-impact paradigm shift that can save not just money but also professional relationships."

**DR. DENNIS MCKEVITT** CRITICAL CARE MEDICINE

# CRITICAL RELIEF

# CRITICAL RELIEF

## A CEO's Guide to Transforming Hospital Culture

DR. MARK MC GINLEY

modern wisdom
PRESS

modern wisdom
PRESS

Modern Wisdom Press
Crestone, Colorado, USA
www.modernwisdompress.com



Published 2024

Paperback ISBN: 978-1-951692-45-2
eBook ISBN: 978-1-951692-46-9
Cover and interior design by KP Books
Author photo courtesy of Stephanie Rau Barber

To those in the healthcare industry inspired
to deliver customer service excellence.

"Clients do not come first. Employees come first.
If you take care of your employees,
they will take care of the clients."

**SIR RICHARD BRANSON**
FOUNDER, VIRGIN GROUP

# CONTENTS

# FOREWORD

**WHEN I FIRST** met Dr. Mark Mc Ginley, I quickly realized that we were singing off the same hymn sheet regarding customer experience. In Dr. Mc Ginley's case, his hymn is tuned to improving the physician-patient experience in the US healthcare system.

My work as the CEO of Customer Service Excellence in Ireland involves many sectors where customer service and customer experience are vital, including telecoms, retail, engineering, hospitality, tourism, financial services, and healthcare, among others.

We first spoke when I was designing and preparing to deliver a patient experience program to administrative staff at the Mater Misericordiae University Hospital in Dublin. The conversation we started then is ongoing in many ways. We immediately understood one another because Mark and I had swapped countries. I was born in New Jersey, USA, and moved to Ireland, where I now live, at the age of eight; Mark was born in Ireland and, via South Africa, moved to the States to practice medicine in 1992. He now lives in Denver, Colorado.

We have spoken at length about the concept of "internal customer service," which suggests that your customer is not first;

your staff is first. In essence, this concept suggests that if we look after our teams, our teams look after the customers.

The heart of *Critical Relief: A CEO's Guide to Transforming Hospital Culture* is rooted in this concept of internal customer service. Inside the pages ahead, Dr. Mark Mc Ginley shares his 30-plus years of physician leadership expertise as he critically examines the patient experience from the inside out. His insights are backed by growing evidence and research to support how a physician-first approach can positively impact patients and overall hospital outcomes.

I am honored to be asked to contribute to this book. Healthcare is one of the world's most important customer experience areas. It is hard to imagine a more vital sector where humans, often at their most vulnerable, require the highest possible level of care and compassion. The author's perspective as a seasoned intensive care physician leader makes the book of even greater relevance.

Dr. Mc Ginley strongly advocates for hospital CEOs to view physicians as "internal customers" who should rise as the primary and most important customers of their organization. He opens a discussion that ignites new thinking and warrants further exploration. The modern healthcare crisis can be addressed by changing a culture that is no longer fit for purpose in a continuously disrupted healthcare world.

Internal customer service and workplace culture are two sides of the same coin. Many sectors are facing a challenge in the recruitment and retention of key staff. Healthcare is at the top of this list. If you are looking for new ways to attract and retain top physicians, the author provides excellent food for thought.

Healthcare organizations that want to thrive must work toward improving their culture and putting key staff—including physicians, nurses, and support personnel—in safe working environments, both physically and psychologically.

Following successful organizations and businesses, healthcare must give greater autonomy to its teams by supporting their development and empowering them with a sense of purpose for the social impact of their vital work.

What I admire most about this book is that it is solution-based. Here is a lifelong physician of standing offering his reflective observations and professional opinions on how vital change is best achieved. I know many CEOs in the healthcare sector who will read this book with interest and an open-mindedness that reflects the importance of Dr. Mark Mc Ginley's thoughts.

By creating communities of best practice and knowledge, and potentially sharing between the US and European models of healthcare, I am inspired to continue this conversation and realize the opportunity we have to enhance the physician-patient experience for the greater good.

As you discover new ideas for positively impacting your organization through *Critical Relief: A CEO's Guide to Transforming Hospital Culture*, I hope you'll be inspired to share this book with others in your organization and industry. Together, we can help in this revolution of change in healthcare—improving the customer experience for administrators, physicians, support staff, and patients across the globe.

*Charlie Boyle*

*CEO, Customer Service Excellence Ireland*

# INTRODUCTION

AFTER A 30-YEAR career as a specialist physician in pulmonary and critical care medicine in the US health-care system, I have an insider perspective on the current healthcare crisis. During my career, I have served in several leadership roles, hiring and managing physicians and working alongside many chief executive officers (CEOs) of small community hospitals, busy urban medical centers, and large university hospitals.

I wrote *Critical Relief* for hospital CEOs and other healthcare leadership to offer a solution to a fundamental issue: the growing exodus of employed physicians from clinical practice. While there are several reasons underlying this crisis, the crux of the problem is the result of poor customer service across the entire healthcare system.

Who doesn't like good customer service? It is many things, but above all, it leaves you feeling seen, appreciated, and understood. It is the magic that keeps us loyal to a company, product, or service. It often manifests in little things like unexpected gestures of thoughtfulness that make your day. It is a level of attention and care that is consistent over time and experienced, no matter which part of the company or organization you might interact with.

Good service turns regular customers into *loyal* customers. In this book, I aim to highlight the experience of one of healthcare's most critical customers: the physician.

As an Irish physician working in the American healthcare system for the past three decades, I see the current healthcare crisis through a unique lens. Growing up in Ireland and South Africa, I was intrigued by the concept of excellence in customer service from a young age. I pay close attention to it whenever I recognize it. I am quick to provide feedback to those delivering it, and over time, I have developed a sixth sense of knowing how to improve it.

Providing excellent service to employees first is the surest way I know to reverse the mass departure of physicians from clinics, hospitals, and healthcare systems across the country.

Most hospital CEOs believe that the patient should be their primary customer. In writing this book, I hope to illuminate the value of viewing their employed physicians as their primary customers. If you provide excellent service to your employed physicians, they will provide superior service to their primary customer, the patient. This, in turn, will improve patient loyalty and the organization's profitability. Improving physician customer service is not cost-prohibitive and can offer a significant return on resources invested.

Hospital CEOs, managers, and administrators must recognize that physicians, as well as patients, are the hospital's customers. Thus, CEOs and other hospital leaders must consider the service experience of their employed physicians. This book is a response to this need.

I also wrote this book for the many other care providers in the trenches. I recognize the stressors care providers battle daily.

You are familiar with the issues I'll discuss in this book. I hope the insights and suggestions presented will help transform your hospital culture, where customer service excellence for all care providers becomes a high priority.

## HOW THIS BOOK IS ORGANIZED

Specializing in critical care medicine has taught me to distill the complex into the simple. Intensivists are generally gifted at cutting through the "background noise" and getting to the heart of the issue. I have tried to do the same with this book. I know how busy you are, so I intentionally wrote this book to take less than three hours to read.

I am not an academic, but I am a physician on the front lines with a background in psychology and business administration. The 11 chapters ahead are my "majors" and, in my experience, represent the core issues—and practical solutions—that matter most to employed physicians.

Together, we'll explore these issues from the perspective of your valued physicians. You'll learn more about my story and what motivates most physicians to ensure high performance and loyalty to their organizations.

You'll gain a deeper understanding of the central issue driving physician burnout and learn how to use motivational interviewing to change behavior and organizational culture. You'll explore new approaches to improving physicians' customer experience in critical areas such as recruitment, onboarding, and orientation. You will also learn about physicians' specific challenges with the electronic medical record and remote management.

Most importantly, you'll be armed with new ideas and practical steps to foster healthy teams and rebuild a culture of transparency and trust, ultimately improving physician retention, patient loyalty, and your organization's profitability.

*Critical Relief* will take you on a paradigm-shifting journey through the eyes of the physician, offering actionable tools for improving your organization's profitability while achieving and maintaining excellence in customer service—for your employees *and* patients.

The physician shortage crisis offers a vital management and leadership opportunity. Artificial intelligence and robotic virtual care will not fix this shortage. Leveraging new technologies will help. However, hospitals and clinics must retain their recruited physicians to ultimately thrive. Physicians will stay with organizations that value their skills, listen to their ideas, and address their needs.

Providing excellent customer service is not difficult when you understand the unique needs of this highly skilled group of employees. In the chapters ahead, you'll get an inside perspective into what makes physicians tick and how to help them *help you* resolve some of your biggest organizational challenges.

Let's get started!

CHAPTER ONE

# THE PHYSICIAN CUSTOMER SERVICE PARADIGM

WINDS OF CHANGE are transforming the US healthcare system. Like the roar of an approaching jet, they've shifted from barely noticeable to unavoidably forceful and pervasive.

As you have likely experienced firsthand, these profound shifts have negatively impacted the doctor-patient relationship and healthcare work culture. The US healthcare system is in a state of crisis on multiple levels, and this crisis has no signs of abating.

Hospital CEOs and those working inside the system grapple with this reality every day. But they aren't the only ones. Patients struggle with hospital care costs, the cost of medications, insurance carrier denials, the inability to afford insurance, the unavailability of doctors, or the high likelihood of having to change doctors every time they change their health insurance.

Healthcare in America is broken, dysfunctional, and in need of change. In these pages, I will provide a road map for what

I consider to be one of the most significant and important changes: customer care to better support doctors so they can better support your patients. It is my firm belief that healthcare organizations that successfully implement this change will not only attract and retain the best care providers but will also deliver outstanding patient care.

## THE BIG PICTURE

The US spends 18% of its gross domestic product on healthcare, nearly twice as much as any other high-income country (Gunja et al. 2023). Despite this, we perform poorly on many metrics of public health. The US has the lowest life expectancy at birth and the highest maternal and infant mortality rates when compared to similar high-income countries throughout the world. And it has the highest rate of people with multiple chronic conditions and an obesity rate of 43%, which is nearly twice the OECD (Organisation for Economic Co-operation and Development) average.

A significant contributor to these problems is a staffing crisis among nurses and physicians that is becoming increasingly bleak. The Association of American Medical Colleges estimates a shortage of physicians between 37,800 and 124,000 by 2034 (AAMC 2021). Any hospital CEO will tell you that the current staffing shortage is the primary driver of escalating labor costs.

The reasons for the physician shortage are numerous. One is the aging of the US population, which suffers from a multitude of chronic illnesses and will have a higher need for medical services as it ages. The aging of the US physician population is another. In addition, the growing exodus of physicians from healthcare due to burnout is unprecedented: an alarming 63% of physicians experience burnout (AMA 2022).

Burnout is merely a symptom of a deeper underlying problem within the current healthcare working environment, an issue that must be addressed for any meaningful change to occur.

## THE PHYSICIAN AS EMPLOYEE

One of the more significant changes in the healthcare environment over the last 20 years is that more than 75% of physicians are now employed by hospitals or corporate entities (Eddy 2021).

Throughout this book, I refer to the published data concerning physicians primarily because I am most familiar with it. I frequently use the word *physician* instead of *care provider* throughout the book. However, what I have to say about improving customer service and experience equally applies to my fellow nurse practitioners and physician assistants.

The values important to physicians and healthcare managers are commonly in conflict. Doctors want to give patients the time and support they need, while hospital administrators prioritize cost containment and productivity metrics. This misalignment of values has alienated an increasing number of physicians from their work.

When surveyed, hospital CEOs overwhelmingly view the patient as their primary customer, with a small percentage listing the physician as the key customer (Mazurenko et al. 2016). But in reality, a hospital CEO has many customers. Financial institutions, regulatory bodies, equipment vendors, physicians, insurance companies, patients, and their families are just a few examples. Trying to satisfy the needs of this diverse group while at the same time meeting the directives of senior management is a difficult and stressful balancing act.

An overarching theme of this book is that to begin to heal the broken system, the physician should be viewed as the CEO's most valued customer.

## THE PHYSICIAN AS CUSTOMER

Hospitals don't have patients—patients are in hospitals because a physician decided to admit them. The physician, not the hospital, orchestrates the patient's plan of care from time of admission to discharge. Yet the physician is increasingly treated by the hospital as a disposable resource. A 2021 survey conducted by the Mayo Clinic found that 20% of 2,900 physicians surveyed had thought about leaving their current practice within the next two years. Why? I believe the answer concerns their experience as hospital employees.

Hospitals are financially rewarded for providing outstanding patient customer service. Conversely, they are financially penalized for inadequate service to physicians through such actions as . . .

- Resignations
- Poor physician retention
- High recruitment and training costs
- High contract labor costs
- Limited physician participation in hospital projects

In addition, several studies have shown a strong correlation between physician burnout and inferior patient care. Poor patient care negatively impacts a hospital's credibility in the community, ultimately diminishing patient volumes.

Centering the physician as a critical customer in a he environment can revolutionize the treatment experie both doctors and patients. Cared-for doctors make for well-treated patients, and patients with positive experiences improve the reputations of the hospitals where they receive their care.

But what I propose will take work. Achieving something of great value usually does. Transforming the customer experience within any organization is fundamentally about changing culture and behavior. In Chapter 3, I will share my techniques to motivate your leadership team to examine its culture and embrace change and improvement.

## MY AIM

I have worked in the American healthcare industry for over 30 years, most of that time as a specialist physician in pulmonary and critical care medicine. I have worked in small community hospitals, busy urban hospitals, and large university hospitals. I have served in a leadership capacity at several of these healthcare facilities and worked with many different CEOs during this time. These varied roles have offered me a ringside seat in the arena of customer experience.

I have always been fascinated by the idea of excellent customer service. Little unexpected gestures and acts of thoughtfulness and attentiveness can transform an everyday experience into something truly memorable. That may be why I studied psychology for three years before answering my inner calling to become a doctor. Regardless of the reason, I am inspired by the delivery of excellent service and admire organizations that ensure a positive customer experience is an integral part of their brand.

In contrast, I have witnessed the destructive aftermath of a community hospital merging with a large healthcare system. The ensuing decline in culture, communication, and physician experience inspired me to write this book. Until now, not much has been published about customer experience in healthcare from the viewpoint of the physician as the customer.

Sometimes it takes a crisis to ignite change. And if you are working in healthcare, you probably feel the rumblings of this ongoing crisis on a daily basis. The problems with staffing burnout and shortages provide the perfect opportunity for hospitals to redefine their primary customer. Changing an organization's culture to respond to opportunities is what institutional leadership is all about.

Hospitals that succeed in providing excellent physician service will lower operational costs and improve the quality of care provided to their patients. Everyone wins.

Let's explore how you can make this happen.

CHAPTER TWO

# MEDICINE

## A Calling, Not Just a Job

MANY OF US who enter medicine feel called in our souls to care for people. The profession is a beautiful mix of altruism, science, and critical thinking. Nothing is more satisfying than knowing you have made a difference in someone's life—a difference that can mean prolonging or even saving that life.

Leaders of healthcare organizations need to know what makes physicians tick. Such knowledge is invaluable in helping hospital CEOs support physicians in their quest to provide the best care possible to their patients. CEOs who truly understand this will be able to create a workplace culture that not only attracts talented physicians but, more importantly, retains them within the organization.

In this chapter, using my own journey as an example, I hope to deepen your understanding of why physicians do this work. It is a glimpse of one physician's nature and inner motivation and a gesture of connection that I hope will benefit you and those you touch.

## MEDICINE: MY UNEXPECTED CALLING

I did not grow up imagining I would become a doctor. I was born in Drogheda, Ireland, a quiet port town on the east coast of the country. When I was three years old, my family moved to the ecclesiastical city of Armagh, Northern Ireland, where my father, Joseph, served as the managing director (chief executive officer) of a shoe manufacturing corporation.

Although both my paternal grandparents were physicians, I had never thought of medicine as a career. However, during our visits to my grandparents' house in Letterkenny, County Donegal, while the adults were engaged in their after-dinner conversations, I would disappear to my grandfather's surgery room at the back of the house to explore his collection of surgical instruments. I would sit at his large wooden desk, with its accordion-like rolltop cover, leafing through medical journals full of anatomical drawings and photos of wounds. It was my favorite room in the house. That was the closest I ever came to medicine as a boy though, and it didn't occur to me at the time that I, too, would become a medical doctor one day.

In 1976, my family immigrated to South Africa due to the troubles that permeated every aspect of life in Northern Ireland, including a depressed economy. I completed high school at St. David's Marist Inanda in the northern suburbs of Johannesburg. I went on to study business administration and psychology at the University of Natal in Pietermaritzburg and secured a summer job at a local hospital. My work as a nursing assistant on the urology ward afforded me the opportunity to meet Dr. Russell Giles.

This experience would change the trajectory of my professional life.

Dr. Giles was a urologist at Grey's Hospital in Pietermaritzburg, the capital and second-largest city in the province of KwaZulu-Natal. As a nursing assistant working on the wards, I took care of simple patient needs, such as making beds and running errands for the nurses. I knew nothing about medicine. For instance, one of the nurses asked me to run to the pharmacy to collect two fallopian tubes. They all had a good laugh when I returned red-faced and empty-handed.

Dr. Giles could see I was extremely interested in the daily rounds he conducted on the ward. I would follow at a distance and pretend to make the beds so that I could listen in. One day, he turned to me and asked, "Mark, would you like to join us?" So I became included in the daily bedside rounds.

A few weeks later, he asked me if I would like to assist him in the operating room with a nephrectomy (surgical removal of a kidney). This experience ignited an inner flame that still burns strong to this day. I wore all the sterile surgical gear and stood on a small stool so that I could see everything. He explained the operation to me in great detail. Afterward, as we chatted in the changing room, he informed me that he had only entered medical school after first completing a degree in mechanical engineering.

"Mark, it's not too late for you to consider medicine as a career."

That was it! This man could see inside my soul. I cycled home as fast as I could and ran into the kitchen to find my father sitting at the table.

"I want to be a doctor," I announced.

But what was it about Dr. Giles that resonated so powerfully with me and opened my eyes to my true calling? I was in awe of how he treated his patients. The respect and rapport he demonstrated with his nursing staff was the best example I had ever seen of teamwork. His communication skills and confidence impressed me deeply. I wanted to do this work with the competence and sensitivity he possessed.

I finished my business degree and was accepted to the University of Cape Town medical school. During my summer vacations from medical school, I kept returning to Grey's Hospital to work with Dr. Giles. But not long after one of my summer jobs, I was devastated to learn that he had been diagnosed with a malignant brain tumor (glioblastoma multiforme). He had to give up the work he loved and was so good at.

The following summer, I sat on the veranda of his house, and we drank a cup of tea and talked about life. As I walked away, I knew I would never see him again. He died a few months later at age 46.

To this day, my approach to patients, their families, and the nursing staff is in no small way a reflection of what Dr. Giles taught me. In particular, to take time with your patients and listen well, learn from your nurses, and constantly seek their input, as they have so much to teach you about your patients.

I graduated medical school in December 1990 and returned to Grey's Hospital to complete my compulsory internship year, a requirement to become officially registered as a physician. It was strange not seeing Dr. Giles there. Still, I could sense his presence everywhere I went. I often found myself in challenging situations thinking, *What would Dr. Giles do?*

I followed my internship with my first junior doctor job at Chris Hani Baragwanath Hospital (the world's largest hospital at that time) in the bustling city of Soweto in the southwest corner of Johannesburg. As a medical officer in the department of surgery, I worked in an extremely busy trauma unit. Friday nights there were the closest I ever came to working in a war zone. One night, we admitted and emergently repaired three patients who had sustained stab wounds to the heart. All three survived and were discharged home!

## MEDICINE AND LIFE IN THE UNITED STATES OF AMERICA

I decided to look into training opportunities in the USA. I was offered a three-year Internal Medicine Residency at MedStar Franklin Square Hospital in Baltimore, Maryland. I asked my then girlfriend, Cathy, if she would marry me and come with me on this American adventure. We arrived in June of 1992 to a sunny and humid city near the Chesapeake Bay. The following year, I had the good fortune of winning a green card in the lottery system administered by the U.S. Department of State. This random event changed everything. We decided to stay and make the United States of America our new home.

That same year brought an experience that would radically alter my perspective. I developed pulmonary tuberculosis (TB) and saw medicine from the patient's perspective.

## I DISCOVER MY SPECIALIZATION

Tuberculosis is endemic to South Africa, and I had cared for hundreds of TB patients. I had even completed an elective assignment at a dedicated TB hospital in Worcester in the rural

Western Cape. When I arrived in the United States, I had been infected but did not yet have the active disease. But the daily grind of my internal medicine residency training had left me exhausted and sleep-deprived. This lowered my immunity and allowed the latent tuberculosis to blossom into active disease.

I was referred to Dr. Marie Chatham, a pulmonologist and critical care specialist. During my ICU (intensive care unit) rotation at Franklin Square Hospital, I had met Dr. Chatham and been impressed by her clinical and diagnostic skills. But more importantly, I admired her poise and grace in the midst of chaos and the sophisticated communication skills she displayed in her interactions with patients and their families. I knew I was in good hands.

I underwent a bronchoscopy. My samples were positive for TB, and I promptly started on antituberculosis treatment. This consisted of weekly intramuscular injections for the first two months and the daily ingestion of a handful of tablets for a total of six months.

My experience as a pulmonary patient and my time working with Dr. Chatham in the ICU clarified what I wanted to do for the rest of my career. I was in my element during my ICU rotation. I found myself immediately drawn to the complexity of the patient's physiological aberrations and the technology employed to care for them.

I had the communication skills to provide relief and understanding to my patients. In addition, I was good with my hands; the technical aspect of doing procedures seemed to come naturally to me. Furthermore, I liked being a generalist. I really enjoyed looking after the whole patient and not just one body system at a time. ICU work would require me to keep up-to-date on all the specialties within internal medicine. This career path would be consistently challenging, and I would never get bored.

Like many big decisions in life, this was not primarily logical and intellectual. My heart and soul were speaking, and this was my passion. I wanted to do this work for the rest of my life. I could not fully articulate why, but I knew it had something to do with the fact that my mother, Imelda, had died in an ICU when I was 19.

I remember vividly how scared and overwhelmed I was by the ICU environment and the ventilator that was breathing for her. She had sustained a spontaneous intracerebral hemorrhage. The ICU physician caring for her brought my father and me into an adjacent room and explained that my mother had sustained a non-survivable stroke. We were then left alone to decide about the next step in my mother's care. We made the decision to stop the mechanical ventilation.

Now all these years later, I was going to become an ICU physician. I wanted to do this work. Not so much because of the intellectual appeal. I wanted, above all else, to be able to help the families of ICU patients feel understood and supported. I wanted them to feel well guided as they negotiated the complex world of the ICU and the roller coaster of emotions that frequently emerge. After all, I knew how they felt. The experience with my mother had, in some unexplainable way, primed me for this work.

My career in pulmonary and critical care medicine began in the summer of 1995, when I was accepted to the Pulmonary and Critical Care Medicine Fellowship Program at the University of Maryland. I graduated from the program in the summer of 1998.

## A WEALTH OF NEW EXPERIENCE

My first job as a pulmonologist and intensivist was at Upper Valley Medical Center (UVMC) in Troy, Ohio, where I served as the Medical Director of the Respiratory Therapy department and Pulmonary Rehabilitation Program. Working with Dr. William Castaldo, I helped UVMC build its first hospitalist program. The development and expansion of this program was a great success, due in no small part to the unfaltering support from the hospital's CEO, David Meckstroth.

I then spent a couple of years in the world of academic medicine as an Assistant Professor of Medicine at Eastern Virginia Medical School. This job required significant teaching and research responsibilities in addition to a heavy direct patient care requirement. However, I discovered I was not good at research. It required a level of patience I did not possess. I was coming home to my young family exhausted. In my heart, I knew this was the wrong career path for me.

## LESSONS LEARNED IN THE MOUNTAIN WEST

A job advertisement caught my eye. It highlighted access to the great outdoors and the beauty of the Rocky Mountains, with the promise that you could "be your own boss." My adventurous spirit was awakened. In July of 2003, my wife, our three children, and I relocated to Casper, Wyoming, where I started my own private practice. I would be working at Wyoming Medical Center (WMC), the largest hospital in the state. Little did I know that this was the beginning of a 20-year career.

Aside from the area's dazzling mountain vistas and the appeal of being my own boss, the real attraction to working at WMC was the person I would share my after-hours call with, Dr. Don Smith. Don was smart, funny, and extremely generous with his time. I really liked being in his company. We trusted and supported each other. Don's deadpan wisecracks punctuated his sharing of a remarkable breadth of knowledge. He took me to lunch regularly and would tell me hilarious stories about personalities that had worked in the hospital since his arrival in the late 1970s. I began to understand the culture of the hospital and how things really worked. Don was respected and liked by administrators and clinical staff alike. He was wise and a great listener. I frequently sought his guidance and advice on matters clinical, financial, and personal.

Eventually, we combined our practices and worked under the same roof. It was hard work. We alternated being on call every other day and every other weekend. We were frequently called into the ICU in the middle of the night to care for an unstable patient.

We did it all—providing outpatient care to patients in the pulmonary clinic, doing inpatient pulmonary consultations, providing care to critically ill patients in the ICU, performing the bronchoscopies required for both inpatients and outpatients, and interpreting pulmonary function and sleep studies.

Don was 16 years older than me, and eventually the time arrived when he wanted to retire. For several years, we tried to recruit a replacement but without success. Then I floated the concept of starting an intensivist program to the hospital CEO and the members of the hospital board. I felt that it was no longer feasible for one person to perform so many clinical functions, and that a division of labor would improve our ability to recruit and also improve the delivery of clinical care.

I'll return to this in Chapter 10, but what's worth noting here is that this was a most rewarding collaborative experience. It gave me a nuanced understanding of how administrators and healthcare providers can draw on each other's strengths to achieve a common objective and improve the healthcare experience for both patients and providers.

In summary, I believe that my story is, in many ways, reflective of most physicians. The decision to become a doctor is an inner calling. This attraction to the field is frequently the result of a personal experience that ignites the inner desire to do this work. Physicians are not primarily motivated by money, and we gain the most satisfaction from spending time with our patients and helping them improve the quality of their lives.

Physicians also gain a tremendous amount of satisfaction from the work environment and the culture in which they work. In the next chapter, I will discuss why providing excellent customer service to employed physicians in this modern work environment is so valuable to both patients and hospitals alike.

CHAPTER THREE

# PHYSICIANS AS PRIMARY CUSTOMERS

DURING MY 30-YEAR journey through the American healthcare system, I have worked with hospital administrators to create a hospitalist program, an intensivist program, an interventional pulmonology program, and a wellness center within an acute care hospital. I have also served as the chairman of the Department of Medicine and, for several years, was an active member of the medical staff development committee and medical executive committee at the largest hospital in Wyoming, Wyoming Medical Center.

## WHY THE CUSTOMER EXPERIENCE MATTERS

You may ask what all of this has to do with customer experience. The answer is *everything*. Having recruited and managed physicians in several settings, I know that those on the receiving end of repeated poor experience in their working environment will eventually leave their positions. This is a deeply troubling and preventable event.

What makes for a good customer experience? We seem to be most aware of this in the hotel and hospitality industry. You notice an attentive employee who goes the extra mile, who is engaged and truly listening. They anticipate your needs and circle back to ensure you are doing well. It is no different in healthcare. For example, when the CEO takes you aside and shares the positive feedback they received about how well you managed a very difficult case in the emergency room the prior week, you feel appreciated and seen. This communication is both unexpected and thoughtful. It also illustrates customer service in action.

The attitudes and behaviors that make one feel seen, appreciated, important, and valuable are not industry-specific. I believe that the features of good customer service in the hospitality industry are equally applicable to the healthcare industry. They represent universal qualities that are at the core of good service irrespective of the industry.

In the world of healthcare, it is common to hear about hospital efforts to improve the customer experience for its patients. The Centers for Medicare & Medicaid Services incentivizes this: it now includes the patient experience in its calculations of a hospital's reimbursement for services rendered. Hospital Consumer Assessment of Healthcare Providers and Systems is one such survey that hospitals use to measure the customer experience of their patients (CAHPS, 2024). Some hospitals have even created the position of Chief Experience Officer.

As of writing this book, there is a movement to expand the customer experience beyond the one-time clinical encounters and engage the patient throughout the continuum of their life. Moving beyond a survey question of "How did we do?" to "How are you doing?" the organization seeks to understand what matters most to the individual in their journey.

Providing a positive patient customer experience is important; however, it is crucial that hospitals shift their focus to the physician as primary customer. With this paradigm shift, not only will they provide better care and be more financially successful, they will also create a workplace culture that attracts, engages, and retains the star talent needed to achieve business success.

## AN EPIDEMIC OF PHYSICIAN BURNOUT

American medicine appears to be at a tipping point, reflecting back to that statistic mentioned in Chapter 1 that 63% of US physicians experience professional burnout. If more than 60% of physicians over a wide range of specialties are experiencing burnout, then we have a systemic problem. Teaching physicians to be more resilient will not resolve this issue. Instead, hospital leadership must examine, understand, and address the organizational factors that contribute to this experience.

For instance, Hartzband and Groopman maintain that the widespread implementation of the electronic health record and performance metrics are the major drivers for the epidemic of physician burnout (Hartzband and Groopman 2020). Some have dismissed the problem as a generation of "dinosaur" doctors whining and pining for an inefficient, low-tech past. However, a growing body of data indicates that millennial physicians, residents, and even medical students are also showing signs of burnout. These radical changes to the healthcare system have left physicians alienated and disillusioned.

According to Hartzband and Groopman, "Solutions have largely targeted the doctor, proposing exercise classes and relaxation techniques, snack and social hours for decompressing, greater access to child care, hobbies to enrich free time, and ways to increase efficiency and productivity. There is scant evidence that any of these measures have had a meaningful impact. These data lead to the inescapable conclusion that currently proposed solutions do not address the underlying problem: a profound lack of alignment between caregivers' values and the reconfigured healthcare system."

## VALUING PHYSICIANS

A mix of altruism and science makes medicine a unique profession. It is interesting and challenging work. You apply your scientific knowledge and problem-solving skills to help people in their darkest hour. You even get the opportunity to save human lives. Thus, doctors commonly derive spontaneous satisfaction from the activity itself—that is, they're intrinsically motivated.

But the current restructuring of the American healthcare system has turned doctors' service into a commodity akin to a product delivered at the end of a production line. This is measured in relative value units (RVUs), number of patients seen per day, average daily census, and numerous other metrics. However, these evaluations and measurements have little meaning or value to physicians, who commonly view them as demeaning and degrading compared to the real work they perform.

For example, what does a hospital CEO mean when they describe Dr. Jones as a great physician? The CEO will not do this because Dr. Jones's RVUs are high or her chart deficiencies are low, no more so than a clinic patient will say she is a great physician because she sees 40 patients per day. Instead, they would say, "Dr. Jones takes great care of her patients. She is smart and really good at what she does. She is compassionate and communicates well with her patients and their families and all the members of the care team." What makes their physicians great will never be found within the pages of a spreadsheet.

In medicine, we get the best results when we can diagnose and treat the cause of the disease, not merely treat the symptoms. The cause of the disease eating away at modern healthcare is the collective disregard for the quality of the physician's experience. Improving the physician customer experience is the single most important activity a hospital or larger healthcare system can do to improve the workplace culture, physician job satisfaction, and the quality of clinical care.

Physicians are inherently critical thinkers and problem-solvers who want to be involved in assessing and improving their practice environment. It does not cost a lot of money for a hospital CEO to develop a relationship with their physicians and seek to understand what matters most to them. The hospital as a whole will benefit if all those tasked with leadership ask their physicians, "What is your customer experience with this organization?" Engaged physicians who are happy working at their hospital don't materialize by pure chance. Healthy environments are more likely to emerge when the organization is actively focused on delivering the best possible service to its primary customer: the physician.

## PHYSICIAN EXPECTATIONS

All those involved in hospital leadership, from CEOs to department managers, must periodically assess the needs of their primary customer. While physicians' specific needs will differ depending on the environment, CEOs can satisfy most of their core expectations by employing what I call the "human skills."

Here I have listed some human skills that hospital administrators can cultivate to establish a positive customer experience and culture for physicians.

- Trust
- Open communication
- Support
- Transparency
- Honesty
- Humility and ownership of mistakes
- Appreciation and acknowledgment
- Engagement

One key CEO action that will go a long way to support physicians is to ask for their input on matters affecting them and their patients *before* decisions are made.

The majority of hospitals and healthcare systems offer their physician employees a fair compensation and benefits package. It is rare for a healthcare provider to leave an employer because of benefits or compensation. However, they will often leave when they do not feel valued. An employer may be able to attract physicians with the benefits/compensation package, but culture and customer experience will retain them.

## BREAKNECK CHANGES IN HEALTHCARE

The rate and extent of change occurring in the healthcare space is profound. Estimates project that medical knowledge doubles every 73 days (Densen 2011). For CEOs and other medical professionals, attempts to keep up with this rapid evolution in clinical care are, at best, incomplete and extremely demanding.

For example, here are just a few changes in my own specialty from 2024.

- Criteria for chest CT screening for lung cancer were revised.
  - Screening should now begin at age 50.
  - The minimum pack-year smoking history requirement has dropped to 20.
- New technology has enhanced the early diagnosis of lung cancer.
  - Robotic bronchoscopy
  - Electromagnetic navigational bronchoscopy
- Physicians can now select the most specific form of chemotherapy for the treatment of lung cancer using biomarkers.
- Endobronchial valve placement is playing an emerging role for the treatment of severe emphysema.

Superimposed on the clinical domain is the never-ending digitalization and computerization of medical practice. The electronic medical record, as we'll explore more in depth in Chapter 7, is now an unavoidable part of medical practice and a constant source of frustration for physicians.

Compounding these issues is a new culture of outsourcing decision-making to a remotely located head office, which sometimes gives the impression of a CEO with limited authority. This creates a buffer between the local administration and physicians, and it hinders transparency and efficiency. However, it is rarely the case that local CEOs are completely powerless to make decisions, and this presents an important customer service opportunity for the local CEO.

Even when a CEO must defer to a remote head office, it is crucial that they advocate for the local physicians. They must frequently update and keep the physicians engaged and informed. Doing so not only builds trust, it also gets to the heart of delivering a great physician service experience. Should the final outcome not be what local physicians were hoping for, the relationship is none the worse, as the trust and respect built along the way remains intact.

## THE IMPACT OF POOR CUSTOMER EXPERIENCE

My guess is that you can recall an experience of poor customer service. Your hotel room has no hangers for your clothes, there is no toilet paper in the bathroom, and the concierge is less than apologetic. You've been waiting for an expensive winter coat to arrive in the mail for a month. It's getting chilly outside! The company offers no phone number and little recourse.

The result of a poor service experience is unmet expectations, disappointment, frustration, and/or a feeling of being unimportant, undervalued, or unappreciated. Similarly, if a poor customer experience is an integral and recurring part of your workplace, then it will ultimately drive you to leave your job and take your talents elsewhere.

And this problem has a big price tag. One of the biggest challenges for hospital CEOs is managing their escalating labor costs. The

Association of American Medical Colleges projected a shortfall of up to 86,000 physicians by 2036. The estimated cost to replace a physician varies between $500,000 and $1 million (Berg 2018).

The reality of the current workforce landscape presents a unique opportunity for hospital CEOs. On the one hand, physicians are a scarce resource in big demand and are extremely expensive to replace. On the other hand, hospital CEOs who truly understand the impact of excellent customer service will retain their best talent, and in so doing, significantly reduce their labor costs while improving the quality of care delivered at their hospital.

## WHY THOSE IN HOSPITAL LEADERSHIP SHOULD BE OPTIMISTIC

Poor customer experience is ubiquitous from the perspective of the care provider. However, you can detect and measure it, and most importantly, use it as the focus to improve the culture of your organization. If you address it successfully, you can significantly improve morale, work culture, and job satisfaction, which would have a subsequent effect on retention rates, quality of patient care, and ultimately, hospital profitability.

Improving customer experience requires more than administering a survey. Seeking to understand, listening, and building trust and rapport require an investment of time. However, this is time well spent, as the return on investment is enormous. It is not expensive to understand the customer experience. A surgical robot will cost a hospital approximately $1 million. But losing the physicians who operate it and eroding the trust of the patients in the community will cost many multiples of this. Tackling this pervasive problem presents a unique opportunity for CEOs to improve their workplace culture, the care they deliver, and the financial viability of their hospital.

Engaged physicians who are satisfied customers deliver better care and have better patient outcomes. Conversely, physician burnout and dissatisfaction are closely related to job turnover, reduced workplace productivity, and reduced quality of care and patient safety.

A study by Firth-Cozens and colleagues found that work-related stress led to 50% of physicians reporting reduced standards of patient care, 40% reporting irritability and anger, 7% reporting serious mistakes not leading to patient death, and 2.4% reporting incidents in which the patient died (Firth-Cozens and Greenhalgh 1997). A two-year study by DiMatteo and colleagues found that physician overall job satisfaction positively impacted patients' adherence to treatment in managing their chronic diseases (DiMatteo et al. 1993). As CEOs know firsthand, retaining the physicians you have recruited at significant expense is good business.

## THE CHALLENGE OF CHANGING BEHAVIOR

Understanding how healthcare institutions can alter their behavior is not so different from considering how we operate as individuals. As a physician, one of my greatest professional challenges is to change patients' behaviors. Getting someone to lose weight, stop smoking, change their diet to improve their glycemic control, or even take their medication as prescribed is easier said than done.

Early on in my career, I believed that a logical presentation of the facts would suffice to change a patient's actions. However, I often found this was ineffective. It was not until I was taught the technique of motivational interviewing that I saw the power of getting patients to verbalize their own thoughts and insights. Behavior is much more likely to change if the motivation comes from within.

Given the success of this motivational interviewing technique in the clinical setting, it should work equally well for the busy hospital CEO seeking to change the leadership team's behavior (Lubman et al. 2012).

I will illustrate the technique by way of an example from clinical medicine and then extrapolate it to improve the service that the organization provides to physicians.

How does it work? The technique explores the three areas necessary to change behavior: **readiness, importance, and confidence**.

• • •

Let's take the example of alcohol abuse.

HEALTHCARE PROVIDER Describe what you like and do not like about drinking alcohol?

PATIENT When I drink, it makes me relaxed and talkative. I feel less reserved and more social. I do not like the way I feel the next day after drinking because I am lethargic and have a headache. I don't feel like I've had a restful sleep.

HEALTHCARE PROVIDER Are there any advantages to changing?

PATIENT Yes. I would lose weight. I would have more energy in the morning to get up and exercise. I would save money. It would be better for my health. I don't want to get dementia.

**HEALTHCARE PROVIDER** On a scale of 1 to 10, with 10 representing your most important priority, how important is it for you to stop drinking alcohol?

**PATIENT** I would say it's a 9.

**HEALTHCARE PROVIDER** What things are more important to you?

**PATIENT** Keeping my job and being able to pay my bills. Improving my relationships with my wife and children.

**HEALTHCARE PROVIDER** What do you imagine will happen if you do not stop drinking alcohol?

**PATIENT** I will continue to feel hungover and terrible after drinking. My health will deteriorate.

**HEALTHCARE PROVIDER** What good things will go away if the alcohol abuse continues?

**PATIENT** My wife may divorce me. I might lose my job. I could become estranged from my children.

**HEALTHCARE PROVIDER** If your best friend was describing your strengths, what would they say?

**PATIENT** That I am generous with my time and resources, hardworking, thoughtful, and intelligent.

**HEALTHCARE PROVIDER** Describe a time when you were pretty sure you wouldn't be able to make a change but surprised yourself by being successful.

**PATIENT** I was a smoker in my teens and early twenties. I never thought I could stop. However, the father of my best friend, who was a smoker, died at a young age from lung cancer. I decided to stop, and I have not smoked since then.

• • •

The key to motivational interviewing is to get the client/customer/patient to verbalize and articulate their own insights and motivation. Behavior change is most likely to occur when the motivation and plan are self-discovered, verbalized, and shared. If one applies this to the scenario of the hospital CEO consulting with their team about how to improve physician customer experience within the organization, it might look like this.

• • •

**CEO** Describe the things you like and do not like about physician service within our organization.

**CHIEF MEDICAL OFFICER/PHYSICIAN PRACTICE MANAGER/PHYSICIAN CHIEF OF STAFF** I like that we offer a competitive salary and benefits package. I do not like that physicians tell me they feel marginalized . . . that their ideas, insights, and opinions seem irrelevant. They feel that many important changes that directly affect their practice of medicine are imposed on them without prior input or discussion.

**CEO** Are there any advantages to changing the physician customer experience?

**CHIEF MEDICAL OFFICER/PHYSICIAN PRACTICE MANAGER/PHYSICIAN CHIEF OF STAFF** Yes. If we improve our physician service, they will feel more valued and aligned with the organization and enjoy a better working environment. This will translate to better patient care, and physician retention rates will improve.

**CEO** On a scale of 1 to 10, with 10 representing your most important priority, how important is it to you to improve the physician customer experience in our hospital?

**CHIEF MEDICAL OFFICER/PHYSICIAN PRACTICE MANAGER/PHYSICIAN CHIEF OF STAFF** 9

**CEO** What things are more important?

**CHIEF MEDICAL OFFICER/PHYSICIAN PRACTICE MANAGER/PHYSICIAN CHIEF OF STAFF** Keeping the lights on and staying profitable.

**CEO** What do you imagine will happen if we do not improve the physician customer experience at this hospital?

**CHIEF MEDICAL OFFICER/PHYSICIAN PRACTICE MANAGER/PHYSICIAN CHIEF OF STAFF** Physician burnout will persist. We will continue to lose great physicians, and our patient care will suffer. In addition, our recruitment and replacement costs will increase exponentially.

**CEO** What things will go away if our current level of physician customer service remains unchanged?

**CHIEF MEDICAL OFFICER/PHYSICIAN PRACTICE MANAGER/PHYSICIAN CHIEF OF STAFF** Our patients will seek care elsewhere. Our reputation in the community for providing great care will diminish. It will also be more challenging to attract new physicians.

**CEO** If your best friend was describing your strengths, what would they say?

**CHIEF MEDICAL OFFICER/PHYSICIAN PRACTICE MANAGER/PHYSICIAN CHIEF OF STAFF** That I always find a way to get the job done. That I am reliable and dependable and that I think outside the box. That I do not give up easily.

**CEO** Describe a time when you were pretty sure you wouldn't be able to make a change but surprised yourself by being successful.

**CHIEF MEDICAL OFFICER/PHYSICIAN PRACTICE MANAGER/PHYSICIAN CHIEF OF STAFF** At my previous job, I had to convince the hospital board of directors to invest in a new building to expand our outpatient endoscopy services. I had to create a business plan depicting different scenarios. I felt totally overwhelmed and out of my depth, but I made the presentation and the board approved the plan.

• • •

Here are eight key questions to use during motivational interviewing.

1. Describe the things you like and do not like about [undesired behavior].
2. Are there any advantages to changing?
3. On a scale of 1 to 10, with 10 being the most important thing in your life, how important is it to change this behavior?
4. What things are more important?
5. What do you imagine will happen if you do not make a change?
6. What things might go away if you continue [undesired behavior]?
7. If your best friend was describing your strengths, what would they say?
8. Describe a time when you were pretty sure you wouldn't be able to make a change but surprised yourself by being successful.

If you really want to improve your effectiveness at behavior change, add motivational interviewing to your skill set. Ask a colleague to interview you with these questions. It is important to verbalize your responses openly. You can apply this technique to any discussion of change to get people to figure out for themselves why the change should happen and how it will benefit them directly. Motivational interviewing is a powerful technique available to all leaders who are serious about culture change within healthcare.

When broken down to the basics, workplace culture is fundamentally about relationships and styles of communication. In the next chapter, I highlight ways in which hospital administrators and physicians can strengthen their understanding of each other and how this can impact customer service within the organization.

CHAPTER FOUR

# BUILDING CONNECTIONS TO REBUILD CULTURE

IT IS ABSOLUTELY possible to rebuild a culture of openness and involvement, and a sense of togetherness. That is what physicians want. Doing this will not cost a significant amount of money. What will it require? Vulnerability and courage.

CEOs frequently feel torn between what the head office and regional managers require from them and what their physicians need from them. But it is essential that hospital leaders cultivate a culture of human connection among the professionals who serve as their key customers. A hospital's physicians must be recognized, heard, and appreciated, since it is their expertise that shapes the quality of care patients receive. And recruiting new physicians into the hospital without eliciting their ideas or involving them in the decision-making process will simply recreate the conditions for them to leave.

## GET TO KNOW YOUR PHYSICIANS

A hospital CEO I know writes himself a to-do list for the next day before he goes to bed.

Item #1 on his list every day, and the first thing he will do when he walks into the hospital, is to spend a full hour rounding on the floors and interacting with the care providers. His daily presence in the patient care areas sends a strong message to the providers that he wants to know their issues, pain points, and frustrations. He wants to hear their ideas and suggestions to improve the delivery of care and their working environment.

Obviously, in a hospital with hundreds of physicians, it would not be possible to get to know them all personally. The point of the exercise is to understand the physician customer experience. It is leading by example. This behavior sends an important message to others in nursing and physician leadership that frontline care providers matter. This fosters a culture of engagement.

Most hospital CEOs I have known genuinely desire to make their physicians feel supported and to help them deliver the best care possible to their patients. Most physicians I know want to have a good relationship with hospital administrators at all levels. So if time does not permit you to get to know your physicians directly via in-person conversations or virtually, via Zoom or Google Meet calls, the next best option is to survey your physicians.

Your survey should measure both burnout and customer experience. The Maslach Burnout Inventory is one validated instrument designed to measure burnout. The version specifically designed for the healthcare industry is the Maslach Burnout Inventory-Human Services Survey for Medical Personnel. I have found that it addresses physician concerns effectively and would recommend it for gathering information. You can find it at MindGarden.com.

Since I am not aware of a validated physician customer experience survey, I have created my own, based on my experience in healthcare and my incessant interest in customer service. I encourage you to use or adapt this when querying physicians in your own hospital setting.

1. Do you receive adequate support from the hospital and its leadership regarding the delivery of patient care?
2. What is your experience with the efficiency of the organization in terms of turnaround time for contracts, recruitment process, and decisions that are important to you?
3. Does hospital leadership meet with you on a regular basis?
4. Are your thoughts and opinions sought out prior to decisions being made that directly affect you?
5. Do you feel your ideas, thoughts, and opinions matter in this organization?
6. Who are the members of your team, and do you function well together?
7. What is the hospital doing well and not so well, and how could we improve?
8. Do you feel your salary and benefits are fair and competitive?
9. Is the bonus system reflective of your efforts?

I would structure the survey questions with a five-point Likert scale. Each survey question is followed by multiple blank lines for comments. Scores can be represented graphically for maximum visual effect, and the comments will provide a most valuable platform for how to improve the physician customer experience.

## MATRIX DECISION-MAKING AND CUSTOMER SERVICE

Many of the large healthcare organizations in the United States have implemented a matrix style of leadership, whereby the recipients of a decision never really know who made it and thus have no idea who is ultimately responsible. The leaders only say something like "The ABC Committee made the decision." While such decision-making and communication may impart a degree of corporate efficiency—as all important decisions are centralized in one place and then disseminated to the various hospitals within the system—it offers an abysmal customer service experience.

Physicians with concerns have little or no recourse, as they would have to speak to the whole committee, which may only meet once a quarter. This process diffuses responsibility since no one is directly responsible.

Here's an example. You have a problem, which you discuss in detail with your chief medical officer (CMO), who says she will discuss it with the CEO and get back to you. Weeks pass with no communication. You ask the CMO about the outcome of the issue. You are informed that "it will be decided when the ABC Committee meets next month" at the head office. Eventually, you get the feedback: what you asked for is not possible. You have no idea who made the decision, and it appears your local CEO has little or no authority in the matter.

Arguably, perception is 90% of the problem. This familiar scenario can be significantly mitigated through transparent actions by hospital leadership. As mentioned earlier, it is critical for the local CEO to explain what they did to influence the decision and to frequently communicate with the physicians about the process and the reasons for the final outcome.

## KNOWING THE CEO

Building trust is a two-way street. Physicians who seek better customer service should make a point to get to know their CEO. Thus, CEOs should encourage their physicians to knock on their door, ask for a personal meeting, or set up a virtual call. Building such relationships really does make a difference.

As an example, I recently had breakfast with a retired pulmonary/critical care medicine colleague and asked him about his customer experience at his Minneapolis hospital. "Excellent. I loved working there and stayed for twenty-five years. I had a personal relationship with the CEO and could walk into his office and sit down and chat about issues and needs. I didn't always get what I wanted, but there was a mutual respect. We communicated frequently and understood each other's perspectives."

Clearly, knowing each other's needs is the first step toward cultivating excellent service.

While feedback from the physician survey data is likely to provide the CEO with key insights and can be a valuable way to connect with and engage physicians, surveys in and of themselves do not improve customer experience. I have lost count of the number of times I have completed a corporate survey with no follow-up or feedback. When this happens, it's clear that employee feedback doesn't really matter to the organization.

The box was ticked. The function was executed. But the opportunity to engage and improve the physician's experience was lost.

The following example illustrates this disconnect and the detrimental effect such an empty gesture can have on customer service.

A hospital I worked at wanted to replace its respiratory therapists with the gastrointestinal (GI) nurses for all bronchoscopies performed in the bronchoscopy procedure room. Respiratory therapists had been assisting the pulmonologists with bronchoscopies since the procedure first started at that hospital in the 1970s. The GI nurses were already extremely busy assisting the gastroenterologists with their endoscopy procedures.

The administration thought it would be more cost-effective to have one group of people assisting with endoscopy services than two different groups. The CMO spoke to all the pulmonologists in our group to get our opinions on this issue and asked, "What are your thoughts about the necessity of respiratory therapists being the ones to assist with bronchoscopy versus having the GI nurses assist you?"

All the pulmonologists surveyed (100%) asserted that respiratory therapists were essential for bronchoscopy procedures. As experts in airway management, their presence was important for patient safety. In addition, they were more familiar with our equipment and instruments and the processing of our samples.

"They are crucial to the smooth operation of bronchoscopy," the pulmonologists urged. "Please do not replace them with the GI nurses."

But months later, with no feedback or discussion in the interim, the hospital replaced its respiratory therapists with GI nurses for the performance of bronchoscopy. Needless to say, this became a huge source of dissatisfaction for the pulmonologists. To them, it appeared that patient care and physician satisfaction were simply not as important as cost containment.

Fast-forward two years: All the pulmonologists had resigned, and the hospital had lost a valuable service line. Patients in that community frequently had to travel out of state for specialist pulmonary care.

This is a graphic example of how not knowing your physicians' needs and the subsequent delivery of poor physician customer service can be damaging to hospitals and patients alike.

The idiom "the buck stops here" aptly describes the CEO's role in physician customer experience. The responsibility for making physician customer service a perpetual focus of the hospital's culture lies with the CEO, as does the passion for its mission and for holding middle management accountable to this culture. If a hospital wants to improve physician customer experience, the CEO must model that behavior.

The first job in the provision of excellent patient care is for the hospital to attract top physician talent. How you accomplish this is the focus of the next chapter.

CHAPTER FIVE

# RECRUITMENT

## The Impact of First Impressions

ATTRACTING TOP TALENT has never been more important than in the 2020s, which is characterized by a national shortage of physicians and high rates of physician burnout. In this increasingly competitive environment, hospitals that provide the best customer experience during the recruitment process will be more successful in attracting the top candidates. If you're a CEO who wants to cultivate a culture of good service toward physicians, an improved recruiting process is an important first step toward that goal.

As you likely know, your recruitment efforts are happening in a workforce whose composition is very much in flux. In 2019, 15% of all active physicians in the United States were from the millennial generation. They are the fastest-growing segment of the workforce and have unique needs and values. In particular, they want to work for organizations that offer emerging technology, work/life balance, a collaborative environment, and frequent feedback on how they are doing (JUCM 2019).

Additionally, the younger the generation, the more likely they are to change companies and explore new opportunities every few years. Microsoft's 2022 Work Trend Index published findings from a study of 31,000 workers in 31 countries. About 52% of surveyed millennial (born between 1981 and 1996) and Gen Z (born between 1997 and 2012) workers were likely to consider changing companies. Conversely, 35% of Baby Boomers (born between 1946 and 1964) and Gen X (born between 1965 and 1980) workers said they were considering a job change (Microsoft 2022).

If you seek to build the longevity of bright new doctors, it's well worth considering the factors that will most likely attract and retain them.

## RECRUITING THROUGH A CUSTOMER SERVICE LENS

Some CEOs may feel that devoting time to the recruitment process is beneath them and should be delegated to others. My experience as a physician job-seeker would suggest otherwise. The jobs I have been most certain about have been the ones where the hospital CEO has extended a personal touch. Your contribution to this process will very likely be the deciding factor for the physician. The candidate will have a much better understanding of the hospital's vision and culture and already feel wanted and valued. They will feel seen and not just perceived as a number.

As a CEO, you have no doubt done your fair share of recruitment. In considering the physician as the hospital's primary customer, you should view the recruitment process as the perfect opportunity to convey to candidates the importance of customer service within your organization. A seamless recruitment process, well-organized from start to finish, will convey this message. Keep customer service in mind as you explore the following 10 activities.

- Advertisement
- Marketing
- Initial call
- Subsequent calls
- Itinerary
- Site visit
- Contract
- Departure
- Follow-up
- Assistance with hospital privileging and credentialing

## ADVERTISING

For the advertisement, consult physicians currently doing the work for the position, since they are your experts and know exactly what to highlight about that job. They can represent the position accurately and will have a sense of what will excite a candidate.

The advertising department needs to spend time interacting with the people "in the trenches" who have experience doing the job and really understand what makes it attractive. This needs to happen BEFORE the advertisement is created.

Before the ad goes to print, the draft must also be vetted by physicians currently doing the job to ensure it hits the mark.

## MARKETING

Marketing has significantly benefited from the advances in technology. The internet has a variety of excellent physician job boards.

A few of the best-known ones are listed below.

- DocCafe.com
- HealtheCareers.com
- LinkedIn.com
- PracticeLink.com
- PracticeMatch.com

Although these technological advances have made it easier to reach physician candidates, experienced marketers still excel at the basics. In a telephone conversation with Wendy Castaldo, senior physician recruiter at Tenet Health, she emphasized the importance of following up on details discussed with a candidate. "Nothing kills a deal like unmet expectations," she reminded me.

Her point is a good one. Once I was on a telephone call with a recruiter about a critical care opportunity in New Zealand. The call ended with them saying "I will send you an email this evening with more details about the job and the community." I waited for weeks but never heard back from them. Needless to say, I lost both trust and interest in the company.

Here is some additional advice from Wendy.

- Timing is everything. If you need a physician in 2025, start looking in 2023. You must be proactive.

- Develop relationships with the program directors at residency and fellowship programs in your state and region.

Physicians in training may be two to three years away from completion, but getting to know them and informing them about your job opportunity can yield significant returns. Your team can present on topics such as résumé writing, contract negotiation, or other topics of interest to physicians preparing to enter the job market.

In 2014, the New England Journal of Medicine (NEJM) Career-Center published an article titled "Understanding the Physician Passive Jobseeker," which summarized the results of a survey of 1,000 physicians. The survey sought to understand the job-seeking behavior of US physicians. The results highlighted a category identified as "passive job-seekers."

Passive job-seekers are not a single block of physicians but a range of subgroups with different levels of activity and interest in employment opportunities. The following three groups of inactive job-seekers, taken together, represent 86% of physicians.

- The TIPTOER: "I am thinking about changing jobs but have only started to network with close associates."
- The EXPLORER: "I am not looking for a new job but would be open to discussing selective opportunities."
- The SUPER PASSIVE: "I am completely satisfied with my current job and not interested in new job opportunities."

I share this with you because you should view every doctor you meet as a passive job-seeker! Never miss an opportunity to showcase your hospital and the job opportunities available. Your foresight and willingness to connect with physicians as potential future colleagues may prove to be the best recruitment strategy of all.

## THE CALL

If you want to attract top candidates, promptness is key. A quick response after a candidate expresses interest sends a message that their inquiry is important and that you have an efficient and responsive system in place.

The person who makes the follow-up call will vary depending on the organization. When I was being recruited to Wyoming Medical Center in 2003, the chief of medical staff called me. After giving me a broad overview of the job, he informed me that Dr. Smith from Pulmonary and Critical Care Medicine would email me to set up a convenient time for a more in-depth call.

The person who makes the first call depends on what type of message you want to send. A call from the hospital CEO sends a very different message than a call from an administrative person from the corporate office who has never set foot in the hospital. The CEO's involvement establishes a personal connection to the physician applicant. It also conveys the importance of their job to the organization's success. Most importantly, this personal touch speaks to the culture of communication within the organization and is an example of service excellence in action.

I have made many recruitment calls and been on the receiving end of many such calls. These are my key points:

- Read the applicant's résumé several times. Make note of their training and career path to this point and any unique skills or experiences they possess.
- If the first call is going to be physician-to-physician, the physician with the most experience in the job should be the one to make the call.

- Block off the time you have scheduled for the call so you will be free of interruptions.
- Talk less and listen more. Ask questions that center the candidate, such as these:
  - What are you looking for in a job?
  - What about this job appeals to you?
  - Tell me about your current job and what a typical day or week looks like.
  - Tell me a little about yourself, your personality, strengths and weaknesses, and your interests outside of work.
- Close with a clear next step. For example:
  - "I think you should come out for a site visit to meet our team and see for yourself what I'm talking about. Is that something you're interested in? [*Applicant responds.*] Great. I will pass this information on to Joan, our practice manager, who will be in contact with you tomorrow. Please text, email, or phone me with any questions that come up prior to your visit. I and the rest of the team look forward to meeting you."

## SUBSEQUENT CALLS

If the whole process is centralized in a corporate office, and the finer details are not in your control, coordination can be more challenging. Immediately after the first call, my next one would be to our practice manager. "Great candidate. She wants to come out for a site visit. I told her you would contact her tomorrow and coordinate details."

Regardless of the process in place, it is important to contact the candidate within the agreed-upon time frame.

Generally, the person making the follow-up call will also be the person creating the schedule for the site visit. This presents another unique opportunity for the organization to distinguish itself through superior service. Attention to detail is key.

- Will they be traveling alone or will other members of their family be accompanying them? Depending on the age of the children, the hospital can provide information on community resources that might be of interest such as daycare, schools, and sporting facilities.
- Do they use loyalty programs for air travel, hotels, and/or car rental?
- Do they (or other members of their family) have any food preferences or intolerances?
- Both parties should provide emergency contact numbers. It is important that they know who to contact and how in the event of a travel delay, accident, family emergency, or other issue.
- Inform the applicant that a full itinerary will follow once finalized.

## THE ITINERARY

The recruitment itinerary requires serious thought and meticulous attention to detail. It should include contact telephone numbers and emails for the key people the applicant will meet during their visit. The most sensible option is to have someone local who knows all the hospital managers create the itinerary.

This task requires a significant amount of coordination. It is important to communicate with the lead physician who will spend the most time with the candidate and to get their input on items to include.

Once the date has been confirmed, that person should contact the CEO and CMO to ensure they will be available, and if not, who from administration can substitute in their absence. As mentioned earlier, your personal involvement with the candidate as the CEO speaks volumes about the position's importance to the organization. If you are not available on the interview day, consider calling the candidate afterward.

## RECRUITMENT DINNER

The recruitment dinner is the least formal aspect of the site visit, but it may be the most influential. It gives the candidate the opportunity to gauge the culture of the organization and the character and values of the people they'll work with.

Start with a list of 10 physicians who would be likely to interact with the applicant in their daily work. Contact all 10 in the hope that three or four will commit to attending the recruitment dinner.

Encourage the applicant to bring their spouse/partner to the dinner. If possible, invite physicians who share personal interests such as fishing, biking, or running with the applicant.

Before WMC was acquired by Banner Health, the CEO or the practice manager discussed financial issues with the applicant on the same day of the visit. Since the acquisition, a Banner Medical Group administrator now handles this. Thus, the applicant may not have the chance to review these details on the day of the visit. However, a Zoom call with a remote administrator can be scheduled and added to the itinerary. The applicant should have the chance to review in detail their base salary, signing bonuses, and benefits as part of the site visit. Not allowing an opportunity for this is simply poor planning. By the time the applicant finishes the site visit, they should have all the important details necessary to make a decision.

At a minimum, a site visit itinerary should include the following:

- A visit with the CEO
- A visit with the CMO
- A meeting with the practice manager
- A tour of the key areas within the hospital for the applicant's specialty
- Time with the lead physician who is performing the job that the candidate is applying for
- A meeting with the chief financial officer (or someone of similar expertise) to discuss the employment contract and benefits
- If the candidate is traveling with a partner or family members, planned activities/experiences to enable them to explore the community while the applicant is busy at the hospital
- Details of the recruitment dinner: time, location, and attendees
- A tour of the community with a real estate agent
- Scheduled downtime for the applicant to explore the area

## THE CONTRACT

The physician employment contract can be anywhere from 30 to 100 pages long and can contain many confusing and difficult-to-understand sections. I have never heard of a physician contract navigator, but if such a person existed, I have no doubt they would be in high demand!

Malpractice insurance coverage and benefits packages are fairly similar across the industry, and as such, offer little value for differentiation. In my experience, what physicians really want are answers to the following questions:

- What is the base salary for the job?
- What percentile is this base salary?
  This relates to provider compensation surveys that are published yearly by Medical Group Management Association, American Medical Group Association, and Sullivan, Cotter, and Associates. Physicians rarely have access to this data. Sharing this with the physician demonstrates transparency and provides an open gesture of trust.
- Is there production compensation, and if so, how does that work (with examples)?
- Is there value/quality compensation for achieving certain metrics, and how does that work (with examples)?
- Is there a signing bonus?
- How much is the relocation expense compensation package?
- Is there a student loan repayment package and, if so, what are the details?

Physicians will shop around. It is not uncommon for them to schedule two to three site visits at different hospitals before deciding which job opportunity to accept. They will compare notes before they finally sign one of the competing employment contracts. Hospitals that devote a significant amount of time to explaining the contract and reviewing the above-mentioned key details will set themselves apart from the competition.

## THE DEPARTURE

At the end of my site visit to Wyoming, we were at the Casper airport when Dr. Don Smith smiled and walked up to my wife and me. "Just wanted to make sure everything went smoothly and to let you know how much I enjoyed meeting you both. If there is anything I can do to assist with your decision-making, please do not hesitate to call me."

Don and I looked each other in the eye and exchanged a firm handshake of connection and friendship. I had an inner sense that this was the job for me. I felt seen, valued, and appreciated. My expectations for the site visit had just been exceeded. That surprise personal gesture at the airport made all the difference. It did not cost a lot of time or money but made a big emotional impact.

Sometimes it's the little things that make all the difference.

I am not suggesting that every applicant has to be personally seen off at the airport! The symbolism and the message conveyed are what's important. A meaningful gesture can be a text or a phone call on the morning of departure. It could be a text to inquire if they made it home safely and restate how much you enjoyed and appreciated their visit. It could even be a follow-up call the next day from the CEO. These little actions create an outstanding service experience and differentiate your hospital and your team from others that don't make as much of an effort.

## THE FOLLOW-UP

It is vital to maintain the connection with the applicant following the site visit. The choice of who makes the call and when is an important part of the recruitment process. I think it should be someone who has met the candidate, not an unknown entity from the corporate office.

All those who spent time with the candidate should review their experience together in a group call or text ASAP, while impressions are still fresh. From my experience, turnaround time for formal written or electronic evaluations tends to be slow, so don't wait for this process to unfold to make a follow-up call to the applicant.

Here's an example of what you might say on that call. "I enjoyed meeting you, and the feedback we have received about you has been extremely positive. Those who have met you think you would be a great addition to the team. I know this is a big decision. Do not hesitate to reach out to any of us should you have any additional questions."

How you word this is less important than the fact that you reconnect in a timely fashion.

## SUPPORT WITH HOSPITAL PRIVILEGES AND CREDENTIALING

An applicant who accepts the offer and signs the contract is still many months away from arriving at the hospital and starting to see patients. They must first negotiate the hospital credentialing and privileging process. This is extremely time-consuming and can generate a seemingly never-ending series of questions and issues to clarify.

However, this is still very much part of the recruitment process. Providing the applicant with the name and contact information of the credentialing expert in your hospital goes a long way to making this process as seamless as possible and presents another opportunity to offer great service.

The physician recruitment process is an unparalleled opportunity for a hospital to make a positive first impression and provide a memorable customer experience. As outlined above, it requires thoughtful attention and coordination to ensure a positive recruitment experience for the applicant.

Hospitals that do this well will attract the best talent in a highly competitive physician job market. Keeping this talent within your organization will be the focus of the next chapter.

CHAPTER SIX

# ONBOARDING, ORIENTATION, AND RETENTION

IN THIS CHAPTER, I reveal how physician onboarding and orientation, when conducted through the lens of excellent customer service, is the hospital's best strategy for improving physician retention.

## ONBOARDING

While new hires manage most of their onboarding remotely through the hospital's portal, this also presents the opportunity for the hospital to demonstrate great customer service. Online onboarding means working one's way through an extensive list of activities such as reviewing hospital policies on workplace violence, compliance to federal regulations, infection control, and patient safety, and learning how to locate hospital manuals. This is a bureaucratic function every new hospital employee must endure—but it's also a time for the hospital to make a great impression.

While the hospital will communicate its mission, values, and culture frequently during the internet onboarding experience, a new hire—occupied with working through compliance and corporate policy items—gets little opportunity to experience the hospital's customer service orientation. However, the onboarding process for personal matters as health insurance, pension contributions, and payroll deductions offers an opportunity for the hospital to show its human side. New hires will have many questions about the best choices for their specific circumstances, so knowledgeable face-to-face support from hospital staff is key.

The seamless blending of digital efficiency with human availability, when required, satisfies a basic human need. We all enjoy the convenience of technology, but sometimes we prefer to speak with a real human being. When a new hire needs help with setting up health insurance or a pension plan, the availability of human contact in real time demonstrates a corporation's culture in action. It sends the message "We place a high value on customer service."

As an example, when I had to sign up for my retirement contributions, the email said I should log in to the website, and the platform would walk me through the process. I wasn't quite sure what I was doing but selected the percentage of my salary I wanted to go to the 401(k) plan and the 457(b) plan. My endeavors led to a most unexpected surprise: I received $0 for my first paycheck. Apparently, I had allocated 100% of my salary to the hospital's 457(b) plan!

## ORIENTATION

Hospitals and practices often dedicate a great deal of planning and time to recruitment but less to orientation. However, orientation provides a new hire's critical first impression of the staff, workflow, logistics, and the living culture of the hospital or clinic. A standardized orientation program is the best way to ensure that each new healthcare provider receives a comprehensive and consistent experience.

Consider the tales of two orientations.

> **ORIENTATION 1** A new physician arrives at the hospital on her first day, excited to start. She will be working as a hospitalist. A practice administrator walks her up to the medical unit and introduces her to the colleague with whom she will be working.
>
> She learns that she is on call on her first day. When she goes to the emergency room to see her first patient, she realizes that her computer sign-in ID does not work.
>
> She gets no information about monthly meetings, important hospital telephone numbers, or even the contact information for the colleagues on her team.
>
> She struggles for the next six months, having to hunt down these details on her own.
>
> **ORIENTATION 2** A physician moves to the new city to start a new job with a new hospital. He arrives at the hospital feeling uncertain about what to expect but is pleasantly surprised by the hospital's efficient, organized, and well-thought-out orientation plan. The medical director of the hospitalist program greets him and takes 30 minutes, in private, to explain the job expectations. He then brings the new physician to the medical unit, where he is introduced to all the members of the extended medical team—other physicians and advanced practice colleagues,

nurses, case managers, and the pharmacist. They all take a few minutes to explain their roles and describe how they can assist him.

He receives a folder that contains a comprehensive list of important hospital telephone numbers, web resources, and other information. He learns that he is not on call for the first week. He has been assigned a light workload that increases incrementally every week over the first month. The team invites him to a meet-and-greet social function in his honor on Friday night at a new bistro in town.

He remains with the organization for the next 20 years.

As emphasized by Henderson et al. in a 2019 *Family Practice Management* article called "A New Approach to New Physician Orientation," high-quality orientation can maximize physician performance and is an important first step in the hospital's ongoing retention effort.

Following are the key takeaways from the article.

**Be deliberate about social engagement.** For example, assign the new physician a peer who can help share insider tips, such as who to contact within specific departments and how to access templates in the electronic health record.

**Create an orientation checklist.** Great checklists incorporate hyperlinks to key documents, policies, procedures, or other resources to augment training. Developing a checklist takes time, but it can be used for years and modified as needed. It is important to solicit contributions and ideas for the checklist from staff. For example, a clinical pharmacist could review hospital pharmacy processes.

**Create an orientation schedule.** Tackle the orientation checklist in multiple sessions so you don't overwhelm the new physician. For example, shadowing clinical peers (volunteers can be solicited ahead of time) can help the new physician learn the daily workflow and how to optimize interaction with the electronic health record. An hour of shadowing every other day in the first week can be priceless to a new physician.

**Complete post-orientation steps.** At the conclusion of orientation, ask the physician for feedback so you can adjust activities and learning opportunities for the next time. Conduct an annual review of the orientation process so you can incorporate changes into the hospital's policies and procedures. I recommend saving these updates to a shared electronic folder. Perhaps most importantly, requesting feedback lets the physician know that the organization values physician engagement.

I cannot emphasize enough the need for this feedback. I have endured numerous onboarding and orientation experiences, and without exception, not once was I ever asked to comment on my experience. But a sincere request for feedback will tell newly hired doctors that their opinions are valued.

## RETENTION

Physician retention is a persistent and growing problem for American hospitals with average turnover in the healthcare industry rising steadily in the past decade. Every CEO knows that finding the talent needed to fill these complex jobs is expensive.

As a CEO, you are well aware of the financial and non-financial costs to the hospital of poor physician retention. Examples of some of these are listed below.

- Recruitment and training costs
- Productivity losses
- Reduced quality of care
- Staffing costs (overtime and fill-in physicians)
- Reduced patient satisfaction
- Poor workplace culture

An obvious reason for a hospital to provide exemplary customer service through onboarding and orientation is to reduce staff turnover. The Human Capital Report 2016 found that retention after three years was 58% more likely when new employees went through a structured onboarding program.

I've seen firsthand the destructive effect of high physician turnover on patient care and customer loyalty. I was taking care of a patient in the ICU who had received intravenous thrombolytic treatment for an ischemic stroke. She also had severe peripheral vascular disease and had been told that she would eventually require bypass surgery to her lower extremities. Her course was uneventful, and as I prepared to transfer her out of the ICU, I remember informing her "You need to follow up with your vascular surgeon in the clinic next month about this issue."

Her reply saddens me to this day. "You know, doctor, I had an excellent vascular surgeon who took great care of me for the last fifteen years. He knew me. We had a great relationship and I trusted him. Now when I go to the clinic, I see a different surgeon every time. I am not going back there. I'm going to see a vascular surgeon in Denver."

Anyone who works in a hospital setting recognizes that low physician turnover is good for hospital volumes and breeds customer loyalty. Patients develop relationships with their physicians and value continuity of care. In addition, low physician turnover is a prerequisite for high-functioning teams, as the success of working groups hinges on consistency and stability. Fragmentation and lack of continuity negatively impact team culture, and temporary team members tend to do the minimum expected. Hospitals must *retain* physicians so they can work together frequently and build the trust necessary to become a proficient team.

On the flip side, poor physician retention undermines a hospital's recruitment efforts, making it exponentially harder to recruit for the advertised position. Losing physicians in noticeable numbers begs the question "Why are so many physicians jumping ship?" Most applicants will see through the standard corporate response: "They all left for different reasons." The smart applicant will personally contact one of the recently departed physicians and ascertain for themselves the true story.

So given the importance of physician retention, what more can CEOs and other hospital administrators do to improve it?

Retention bonuses are a short-term fix that are unlikely to have a sustained effect. Physician retention is all about relationship-building. It takes time, but the return on investment will be low physician turnover and a satisfied care provider.

Physicians tend to leave hospitals where they are treated like commodities; where their input, if sought, does not matter; where they experience little transparency or trust; or where all important decisions are made states away.

As an example, when our hospital was taken over by a corporate healthcare system, physician executives from the corporation's out-of-state regional office now managed physicians, instead of local managers doing it. This created a lack of transparency and a lack of trust. It's hard to build a relationship with managers you only see once or twice a month and who don't live in the community or work in your hospital.

In essence, high physician turnover is a red flare across the corporate bow that signals a need for an emergency intervention, without which the ship is likely to sink.

So what does the intervention look like? Does it have to start at the very top of the organization and work its way down to the smallest hospital in the system?

Answering the second question first, the answer is no. Any CEO has the potential to improve the experience of physicians working in their hospital. Spending the first hour of each day rounding on the units and interacting with your care providers does not require a directive from head office. A CEO has countless ways to cultivate a healthy relationship with physicians—I shared some of these in Chapter 3.

To answer the question about what the intervention looks like, a change in mindset is needed. The internal dialogue of this mindset involves continuous reflection on the following questions:

- What are our physicians' pain points?
- How can I improve the service and customer experience for our physicians?

If you start by building relationships with your physician community, you'll easily find the answers to these questions.

The next chapter will explore ways in which hospital CEOs can improve the physician customer experience with the electronic medical record, a major and recurring pain point for many physicians.

CHAPTER SEVEN

# THE ELECTRONIC MEDICAL RECORD

ANYONE WORKING IN a hospital setting is likely familiar with the electronic medical record (EMR). Many of us know firsthand its inherent capacity to madden and exhaust the user.

The EMR industry has expanded rapidly, growing from nearly nonexistent in 2000 to being worth more than $31 billion a year in 2018. In 2009, the United States government allocated $27 billion for hospitals demonstrating "meaningful usage" of EMRs via the American Recovery and Reinvestment Act (Nguyen et al. 2022). It was not possible to meet the meaningful use criteria without adopting EMRs, so as of 2021, 96% of all nonfederal acute care hospitals and nearly four out of five office-based physicians have implemented a certified EMR (Diaz 2023).

To meet the meaningful use criteria, a hospital's EMRs had to encompass the following:

- Clinical data registry and reporting cases
- Exchange of health information

- Coordination of care due to patient engagement
- Patient-provider access
- Computerized provider order entry
- Clinical decision support
- E-prescriptions
- Implementation of protected health data

Presented as an all-in-one miracle, EMRs promised to do the following:

- Reduce medical errors
- Improve patient care, communication, and efficiency
- Develop data repositories for research
- Reduce costs
- Increase patient, staff, and provider healthcare experience and satisfaction

Clearly, this transformation would not have happened without the economic incentive from the US government to do so. The Centers for Medicare & Medicaid Services was empowered to penalize healthcare organizations with a 1% reduction in their Medicare reimbursement if they did not meet the meaningful use criteria by 2015. As many hospitals operate within a 1% profit margin, this represented a meaningful penalty.

The pressure worked, and EMRs are here to stay. However, this technology is in need of dramatic improvement as it has failed to deliver on many of its touted advantages.

## THE UNINTENDED CONSEQUENCES OF EMRS

While EMR technology was intended to help doctors, in reality, it added to their stress and discontent. A 2016 survey of 6,375 doctors in the United States, published in *Mayo Clinic Proceedings*, found that physicians who used EMRs reported feeling less satisfied with the amount of time they spend on clerical tasks. They were also found to be at a higher risk of professional burnout (Collier 2017). A smaller study from 2014 involving 370 primary care providers in New York City had similar findings. Physicians who reported moderate use of EMRs were less satisfied with their jobs and had higher levels of stress (Collier 2017).

According to research conducted by the RAND Corporation, a nonprofit think tank, problems expressed by doctors using an EMR included nonintuitive interfaces, information overload, low-quality documentation resulting from template-based notes, and the lack of interoperability between electronic systems. Some physicians reported working longer hours because of EMRs, with many needing to complete their clerical work at home during evenings or weekends (Collier 2017).

In my opinion, these systems are designed to make billing easier, not to make clinical care more efficient. With EMRs, I spend more time facing the computer than I do interacting with my patients. I make more mistakes now than when I was practicing medicine in the pre-EMR era. For example, I order the wrong lab test for reasons such as these:

- The test I think I am ordering is actually something different within the computerized ordering system (which is not visible to me).
- The dose or frequency of a medication is wrong because the computer defaults to undesired presets.
- I order the wrong imaging study because what I really wanted was not on the drop-down menu, and no one has read the comments that I attached to the order.

- I add notes to the wrong patient's records because I had two different charts open at the same time and became distracted.

We all know the high stakes of our work. Errors in clinical medicine can result in patient harm and even death. The 1999 report by the Institute of Medicine "To Err is Human: Building a Safer Health System" revealed that as many as 98,000 patients die from preventable medical errors in US hospitals each year (Kohn et al. 2000).

EMRs must be frequently revised and updated to avoid unintended errors, which happen regularly as a result of new technology. For example, I was asked to perform a thoracentesis (a procedure where a needle is inserted through the chest wall into the pleural space to remove fluid for analysis) on a patient with a pleural effusion. He had already undergone a thoracentesis three days earlier that had showed no evidence of infection, but fluid analysis suggested he might have lymphoma. The patient was doing well clinically and was to be discharged to go home later in the day. I explained to the patient that I needed to obtain additional fluid for a study called flow cytometry. I obtained informed consent from him, and the procedure was uneventful. I placed the order for flow cytometry in the EMR. The patient was still discharged later that day.

I kept checking the EMR for the results, since I wanted to get back to the patient ASAP. After two weeks passed with no results, I phoned the pathologist. She explained that when a patient is no longer in the hospital, the computer system cancels all orders. She added, "This is a recurring problem, and I have been trying for years without success to get this fixed."

As a result, the patient would have to come back for another thoracentesis. This was an invasive procedure, not without risk. It would cause inconvenience and probably require an additional medical bill for the patient. I had to make three different phone calls until I found a "physician champion" on the EMR upgrade team, who said he would bring this up at the next meeting.

Since these types of rebuild/redesign issues are frequent and never-ending, hospitals must have a local, easy-to-contact team that can promptly address EMR issues that directly contribute to poor patient care. I am hopeful that the advances in artificial intelligence will put the EMR in a position to deliver on its hype.

Until then, however, poor EMR training for physicians is to blame for a good deal of their confusion with the technology—as well as a perception of poor customer service. This problem was the focus of an article published in the *Journal of the American Informatics Association* (Gui et al. 2020). The main challenges from an EMR launch with a large healthcare system in Michigan were as follows:

- Inappropriate training prior to the go-live date
- Insufficient at-the-elbow support after the launch
- Communication challenges with the EMR builders
- System design flaws after the launch

Humphrey-Murto documented another EMR go-live in Canada with a happier outcome (Humphrey-Murto et al. 2023). A participant in that study, who did actually receive peer-to-peer support, exclaimed, "They taught me the things I actually needed to know."

Given universal physician frustration with the EMR, and its association with workplace stress and physician dissatisfaction and burnout, what can CEOs and their leadership teams do to improve what amounts to extremely poor customer service?

Here are a few practical solutions:

- Develop an in-house rapid resolution team that can provide 24/7 support to physicians who need immediate help. The current health information technology system of support is largely ineffective.
- Provide peer elbow-to-elbow support. In-person contact is a must for EMR training. Teach physicians what they actually need to know. Assigning non-physicians to teach physicians is ineffective yet all too common. Also, physicians assigned to provide this elbow-to-elbow support must be from the same specialty.
- Identify physicians from multiple different specialties who are effective EMR users and incentivize them to become peer-to-peer trainers.
- Know the needs of your customers and tailor the training to meet those needs.
- Obtain feedback about your service. Keep improving the training based on that input.

As a CEO, you may cringe at the thought of investing in yet another program. But the costs of implementing these much-needed customer service improvements to the EMR experience will be well worth it in terms of improved efficiency and reduced stress/frustration among employed care providers.

I suspect many CEOs in large healthcare systems struggle with how to communicate and implement head office directives that seem "ill-suited" for the hospital they manage. The next chapter will illustrate ways in which CEOs can address this problem to strengthen the relationship with their employed physicians.

CHAPTER EIGHT

# COPING WITH THE HEAD OFFICE

AS MORE HOSPITALS become part of large healthcare systems, important decisions tend to be centralized in head office departments. Although these silos of authority offer organization and consistency, a corporation with rigid, centrally located divisions can also create a culture of inefficiency, a lack of transparency, and the inability for local leaders to make critical decisions.

You know your hospital has this problem if you hear providers complain, saying things like . . .

"My opinion doesn't matter."

"Nothing ever changes."

"They just don't care."

"No one can give you a straight answer."

"Can anyone around here make a decision?"

And make no mistake: this is a serious problem.

In his book *If Disney Ran Your Hospital: 9½ Things You Would Do Differently*, Fred Lee talks about the glacial speed of simple decision-making in many large organizations and the negative effect this has on customer service and experience. He also highlights the positive impact that occurs when an organization pushes decision-making and problem-solving closer to the front lines (Lee 2004).

## HOW REMOTE MANAGEMENT FAILS PHYSICIANS

A pulmonologist colleague of mine had been employed for almost 11 years at the Wyoming hospital where I worked. Board-certified in internal medicine, pulmonary disease, critical care medicine, and sleep medicine, she was also medical director of the ICU. She was emotionally and physically exhausted from two years of caring for critically ill patients during the COVID-19 pandemic.

"Mark, I need to stop working the night shift and achieve a better work/life balance," she told me one day during patient sign-out.

She was working 100% of her time in the ICU. She wanted to have more time in the outpatient clinic and less time dealing with critical patients. Another physician in our group had already been splitting their time between these two departments for the past two years. This arrangement was acceptable to all parties. In fact, it was a win-win: the pulmonary clinic needed more help due to a massive backlog of patients. In August 2021, one of the healthcare system's financial administrators informed her that a contract would be forthcoming.

September, October, and November came and went. By the time mid-December arrived, still without a contract, she felt unimportant and frankly disrespected. Not surprisingly, she handed in her resignation.

A neurologist colleague informed me that he had been waiting for six months for a contract, for provision of neurology services, from the head office of our hospital's healthcare system. A Harvard-educated Rhodes scholar, this specialist was also a recipient of the American Heart Association's Physician of the Year award. As chief of medical staff for two years at our hospital, he had single-handedly built up an electronic stroke service that served the entire state. He, too, felt invisible to the new hospital leadership. *They just don't care* was his frequent assessment. After six months of waiting for a contract, he also resigned.

When a third member of our intensivist team gave her notice of resignation in March of 2022, I agreed to serve as ICU medical director. The contract was basic boilerplate, delineating standard duties and responsibilities and a single attachment for pay rate. It took five months for my contract to arrive. This was not enough to make me resign, but I felt invisible and unimportant to the healthcare organization.

This is what poor physician customer service feels like. Efficiency matters. Ideally, local hospital leadership should have the authority to influence and expedite the process. When significant decision-making occurs in-house, it is possible to bring an issue up with the local CMO or CEO and receive a response within a reasonable period of time.

## HOW CEOS CAN NAVIGATE REMOTE MANAGEMENT

Perhaps you are struggling with communication issues similar to these at your hospital. Almost every request has to go up the corporate chain for review, usually by people who have neither lived in the community nor worked at the local hospital. This dynamic exemplifies the term "lost in translation." At worst, you may feel transformed into a simple courier of information up and down the corporate ladder.

In situations where systemic takeovers have disrupted individual hospitals' internal communications, it makes a lot of sense to implement measures to ensure some decentralized decision-making authority. Local CEOs can, in fact, do this without disrupting the corporate chain of authority. In many cases, less disruptive changes can maintain the advantages of these specialized silos while simultaneously delivering a much-improved customer experience. Centralized and decentralized decision-making do not have to be mutually exclusive. A hybrid system that employs both ensures superior service for the healthcare organization and its primary customer, the physician.

Here are some examples of how local and remote management can work together for better physician customer service.

- Physically or virtually deploy silo staff to a local hospital during a recruitment crisis.
- Set up a temporary task force of people from the central headquarters to focus on prompt approval and delivery of physician contracts to the local hospital. This will not only expedite turnaround; it will also deliver a strong message of physician appreciation and acknowledgment.

- Have an in-house benefits navigator to help facilitate the onboarding experience and make it more pleasant for new physicians.

Where there is a will to improve customer service, there is a way—even in the presence of centralized silos. When physicians feel supported within the system, the ripple effect is felt throughout the teams that directly and indirectly interact with these care providers. We'll explore the importance of healthy teams next.

## CHAPTER NINE

# NURTURING HEALTHY TEAMS

MODERN HEALTHCARE AND the word *team* have become synonymous. The Resuscitation Team, the Rapid Response Team, the Emergency Room Team, the ICU Team, the Administration Team—the list goes on.

Healthcare is increasingly a team sport, and great clinical care requires the integration of multiple teams. Great customer service is no less of a team sport. Care providers and administrators frequently find themselves on the same team. The focus of this chapter is to help busy CEOs create and develop teams that are not only effective but also provide excellent customer service to the hospital's primary customers, the providers of clinical care.

Good outcomes in medicine, like in business, result from team effort.

Physicians are very comfortable working in clinical teams. A critically ill trauma patient who recovers sufficiently to be discharged from the ICU has in all likelihood been managed by teams made up of emergency room physicians and nurses, trauma surgeons, anesthesiologists and operating room nurses, ICU physicians and nurses, pharmacists, respiratory therapists, diagnostic and interventional radiologists, nutritionists, physical therapists, and possibly other medical and surgical subspecialty physicians. In addition, all these care providers depend on the smooth functioning of additional teams such as radiography technicians, phlebotomists, lab technicians, and members of the case management team.

I suspect we all have, at some point in our careers, observed or experienced a high-functioning team in action. You know it when you see or experience it. While each one is unique, most high-performing teams can be characterized by the following characteristics:

- A common goal
- Trust and respect
- Effective and timely communication
- Effective conflict resolution
- Clear roles and responsibilities
- Strong leadership

I also suspect we have all experienced ineffective, dysfunctional teams. These can be characterized by lack of trust, infighting, poor feedback communication loops, inconsistent support for fellow members, confusion and lack of clarity about roles and responsibilities, and poor leadership.

## ENGAGING POSITIVELY AS A TEAM MEMBER

This chapter focuses primarily on how hospital leadership can best support teamwork among their healthcare providers. But as professionals, we are all individually responsible for contributing our best effort as part of a team. Before we move into group issues, it's worth addressing the ways our biases and emotions can affect team dynamics.

Before participating in a team meeting, I make a point of taking a few deep, cleansing breaths and pausing to assess my mindset. I use the acronym TEAM—for trust, empathy, attention, and mutual support—as a useful checklist.

**TRUST** You want people to trust you and vice versa. Honesty and transparency are necessary to build trust. The more you can trust the other members of the team, the more forthcoming you will be. Do what you say you will do.

**EMPATHY** We all come to the table from different professional and emotional experiences. Seek to understand the WHY behind the other person's viewpoint and what it must be like to deal with their unique issues.

**ATTENTION** This is just another way of saying listen more and talk less! Understand the message behind the words. Summarize the other person's viewpoint and repeat it to be sure you've grasped it accurately.

**MUTUAL SUPPORT** We are a team. We have each other's back. We have to depend on each other, and each of us has to pull our weight for the team to function most effectively. Show support to the other team members.

Just because you participate in a Microsoft Teams or Zoom or Google Meet call does not mean you are a team. The platform a team uses to communicate is no guarantee the team will function effectively. Effective teams need consistency, repetition, and continuity to build trust and patterns of excellence.

## THE NEED FOR LEADERSHIP TRAINING AND DEVELOPMENT

While physicians are specifically trained to function well in clinical teams, they have little or no training in how to lead in the nonclinical arena. Yet physicians are often asked to join teams with healthcare administrators and find themselves in team leadership positions with little or no training. To capitalize on the competencies physicians do bring to their teams, they need support to develop these skills.

One way to help physicians accomplish this is to tap into existing physician leadership training programs. Some of the better-known courses are listed below.

- American Association for Physician Leadership
- Cleveland Clinic's Samson Global Leadership Academy
- Duke Regional Hospital (Durham, NC)
- Harvard School of Public Health's International Leadership Development Program for Physicians (Boston, MA)
- National Center for Healthcare Leadership (Chicago, IL)
- Northwestern University Kellogg School of Management's Physician CEO program (Evanston, IL)
- Penn State College of Medicine's Leadership Academy (Hershey, PA)

For a rigorous academic assessment of the merits of various training programs, please refer to Jan Frich's article in the *Journal of General Internal Medicine* "Leadership development programs for physicians" (Frich et al. 2014).

Many large healthcare corporations have their own internal leadership curriculum and offer quarterly workshops on essential leadership skills. If such resources exist, encourage physicians serving in leadership positions to take advantage of them.

At a minimum, all physician leaders working in teams should complete a basic curriculum of reading. Here are three books I highly recommend.

- *A Culture of High Performance: Achieving Higher Quality at a Lower Cost* by Quint Studer
- *Hardwiring Excellence: Purpose, Worthwhile Work, Making A Difference* by Quint Studer
- *Practicing Excellence: A Physician's Manual to Exceptional Health Care* by Stephen C. Beeson, MD

Regardless of the program selected, leaders and management should support physicians who agree to serve on teams and help them grow and develop their leadership skills. Enrolling physicians in leadership development courses will not only improve their effectiveness within the team, it will also help them feel valued and thereby provide them with a richer customer service experience.

## USE TEAMS TO BUILD RELATIONSHIPS

Many physicians just want to be left alone and minimize their dealings with hospital administration. They want to provide great care to their patients while applying themselves wholeheartedly to their profession. This is understandable. Taking on projects and leading teams is not only time-consuming; it is also likely to reveal their poorly developed leadership skills. However, participating in a team is almost an inevitable rite of passage in the current healthcare environment. Part of being a professional is speaking up and fighting for what we feel passionate about. This typically produces a "Please become a member of Team ABC" invitation from hospital administration.

Most teams form to address a specific and measurable objective within a defined period of time. This work will inevitably require the expenditure of hospital resources. As such, the creation of a team comprising administrators and physicians presents an opportunity for the organization's culture to reveal itself. Thus, a team presents the perfect forum in which to model the values that the organization embraces.

Physicians don't always possess the financial and management expertise required to run a hospital or healthcare system successfully. Similarly, CEOs are frequently unaware of the day-to-day challenges physicians face in the provision of clinical care and the importance of shared decision-making as it relates to clinical excellence and physician job satisfaction.

So is it possible for physicians and hospital administration to work together as a high-functioning team, given that their values may not be in alignment? I truly believe the answer is yes. In fact, team projects offer a powerful opportunity for the two sides to gain a better understanding of each other and, perhaps most importantly, to win each other's trust, which is gained in drops but lost in buckets. One of the most under-appreciated attributes of a high-functioning team may be its capacity to transcend the trust gap between hospital administrators and physicians.

The cultivation of trust and a respectful relationship between healthcare administrators and physicians is another important aspect of a positive customer experience. However, participation in a team is a double-edged sword. Low emotional intelligence and poorly developed leadership skills can give rise to hurt feelings and lost trust among team members. Conversely, strong leadership skills coupled with the display of high emotional intelligence can bring out the best in team members and improve the team's productivity, while at the same time acting as a catalyst for trust and respect.

Physicians who feel valued and appreciated for their participation in a team are likely to communicate their insights and understanding to their colleagues within the hospital and the outpatient offices. This is an extremely credible and powerful way to improve the understanding and cooperation between those who deliver care and those who administer it. This, in my opinion, is how a CEO transforms the workplace culture from a set of values on a poster to a tangible lived experience.

Given the poor understanding of the challenges and frustrations of each other's jobs, the more personal the interactions CEOs and physicians can experience around shared issues, the more likely they are to develop an improved respect and appreciation for each other. CEOs determined to improve their workplace culture will go the extra mile to engage physicians in the development of teams.

## IMPROVING HOSPITAL SYSTEM TEAMS

Administrative decision-making teams in hospital systems tend to be siloed with little physician input. These teams are likely to include a physician at a local hospital who participates remotely in discussions with physicians from several other hospitals within the healthcare system. This team functions more like a committee in which everyone casts a vote, then promptly moves to the next topic.

The efficiency of this structure is obvious from the perspective of a large multi-hospital healthcare system. The structure and function of such "teams," however, fall short in several respects. First, they raise many issues that don't apply to all hospitals in the system, so large swaths of conversation are of little relevance to numerous participants. Second, local issues often require a local solution, which is impossible to develop in this setting. Third, because of these issues, such forums are a poor investment of time and do little or nothing to improve participants' relationships with the leadership at their local hospitals. Improving the workplace culture at your local hospital demands local engagement.

When local administrators provide local physicians meaningful opportunities to participate in the design, implementation, and evaluation of hospital initiatives, all parties benefit. Active engagement of physicians in the shaping of results increases the odds of buy-in. This, in turn, increases the likelihood of improved communication of hospital issues among the local medical staff.

In the next chapter, you'll see how this plays out in one of the most critical areas of a hospital, the intensive care unit.

CHAPTER TEN

# THE INTENSIVE CARE UNIT

## A Case Study

THE INTENSIVE CARE unit (ICU) is the glue that holds a hospital together. If ICU care is good, it will have a positive ripple effect on many other clinical areas within the hospital.

In this chapter, I share the story of a high-functioning ICU that enjoyed a strong culture of teamwork and cooperation. This is a specific and unique story, but it exemplifies the best outcomes that emerge from skillful communication between physicians and CEOs. This exceptional unit came to exist because the physicians who conceived of it were heard, their views were respected, and their perspectives were understood to be pivotal to the well-being of the unit and of great use to the hospital as a whole.

This case study is intended to exemplify the principles explored in this book and how well they can work in action. Unfortunately, it is also a cautionary tale about how poor physician customer experience can impact a fragile ecosystem like an ICU.

## A BRIEF HISTORY

The 14-bed ICU was multidisciplinary—this team cared for critically ill patients from all specialties. It provided ICU support to those in need of complex cardiac, trauma, medical, neurological, cardiothoracic, and vascular surgical treatment. The specialist in critical care medicine, an intensivist, saw the majority (more than 80%) of patients admitted to the ICU. At this hospital, all the intensivists were board-certified in pulmonary and critical care medicine. Prior to the changes described below, only two intensivists (Dr. Don Smith and myself) cared for patients admitted to the ICU. We would take night calls from home, and during the day, we spent a significant amount of our time in the outpatient clinic caring for patients with pulmonary disease.

In 2009, I helped build the hospital's intensivist program with the support of their administration and board of directors. I served as the medical director of this program for the first six years of its existence. Working closely with the CEO, I recruited a team of five intensivists to staff the ICU. The strength of this new model of care was that an on-duty intensivist would be in-house 24/7. Each shift would be 12 hours, with one person doing the day shift and another person doing the night shift.

The work cycle consisted of working two weeks of day shifts followed by two weeks of vacation, which was followed by two weeks of night shifts and a two-week vacation before the whole cycle repeated itself.

## ADVANTAGES FOR ICU PHYSICIANS

From an intensivist's perspective, this model provided an excellent work/life balance. You worked hard for two weeks, but you also had two weeks' vacation every month. This opened up time for family and other enriching activities outside of the workplace. If needed, you could trade blocks of work with your colleagues and have additional time off. You were guaranteed a period of time to rest and recover from the demanding 12-hour ICU shift. In other words, when you were off, you were off: when you signed out, you could turn off your beeper and would not be called back to manage ongoing patient care issues.

You worked as a team and could share ideas with the colleague you were paired with on the other side of the 12-hour shift. You assisted each other and stayed longer, if needed (for example, to help manage an outstanding issue so your colleague could immediately attend to an unstable patient). At change of shift, we walked around the ICU, gave a verbal report about each patient, and discussed the plan of care with each ICU nurse. We supported each other and, over time, our practice styles became similar. You trusted that your patients were in good hands until you returned to start your next shift.

## ADVANTAGES FOR PATIENTS

This model provided a never-ending cycle of care with numerous benefits. Nurses, patients, and their families got frequent updates from the intensivist throughout the course of the day. Patients were re-evaluated frequently. The intensivist facilitated ongoing communication with other specialists on the case and ensured that urgent issues were not delayed. In-house intensivists also functioned as a de facto palliative care service. They brought much-needed support and assistance to patients and families struggling with difficult decisions related to end-of-life care.

## ADVANTAGES FOR NURSES

For nurses, the availability of an in-house intensivist 24/7 was a big source of job satisfaction. The model provided consistency and ongoing continuity of care. Patients received prompt expert care when needed: an intensivist was readily available to perform endotracheal intubation or to place a hemodialysis catheter, a central venous line, a chest tube, or whatever else needed urgent attention. Nurses readily expressed their appreciation for the support this model provided them. An example of this is the following letter addressed to our group from one of our ICU nurses, who left our hospital to work in a large metropolitan ICU in another state. I have abbreviated the original letter but kept parts that illustrated what made the intensivist service important to nurses.

• • •

> Intensivist Service 02/23/2022
>
> I now know what the gold standard of care looks like and, having learned from the best, I will be a much stronger nurse and nurse practitioner in the future.
>
> I have not encountered intensivists that do everything you do. The intensivists I have worked with at other hospitals typically rely on others to do lines, never do arterial lines, and wait for the PICC team even if someone is on a decent dose of norepinephrine. They put a palliative care consult in rather than having that discussion in the moment it needs to happen, and thus delay/prolong suffering. They get cardiovascular surgeons to perform percutaneous tracheostomies and chest tubes. They get anesthesia to intubate depending on the MD, etc. They do not respond to

rapid response codes or medical alerts (Code Blue). YOU DO IT ALL and beyond in a timely manner with a much heavier workload.

I admire your willingness to always put patients and staff first. You all genuinely listened to nurses for concerns, questions, recommendations, etc. You responded as quickly as possible, even when you were in the middle of something or sat down for the first time that day. You made me and many others feel valued and respected back. You all always communicate with us, make sure we know what is going on and what the plan for that patient is.

Speaking of, I know interdisciplinary rounds are stressful for all of you because you are busy doing your own rounds, but thank you for being present for those. I cannot tell you how much it means to nurses, families, and other team members. Our rounds are a joke where I am, and I miss having everyone on the same page.

I cannot tell you how many times I have literally had to BEG for simple standards of care that none of you would question but simply expect. I have now seen good practice and bad practice, and you do not always appreciate one until you experience the other.

Please take care and do not lose hope. You are all heroes—every generation looks up to you. I will never forget what you have given me.

Sincerely,
Jamie Rhodine, RN, BSN, CCRN

## ADVANTAGES FOR OTHER PHYSICIANS

From the perspective of other physicians working elsewhere in the hospital, having an intensivist in-house 24/7 was frequently referred to as "one of the best things about working at this hospital." General surgeons, trauma surgeons, and neurosurgeons could leave the hospital with peace of mind knowing that their patients would be well cared for in their absence.

In fact, the cardiothoracic surgeons and the intensivists worked so closely together that the cardiologists only got involved with a patient's care once the patient was transferred out of the ICU to the cardiology unit.

Hospitalists had a 24/7 expert in-house resource to help care for their complex patients. If a patient on the medical/surgical unit was not doing well, the hospitalist could call or pop in to the ICU any time of day and night and discuss the details with the intensivist.

ER physicians frequently called the in-house intensivist for an opinion about a clinical issue or asked them to come to the ER to evaluate a patient who worried them. Similarly, family practice residents would frequently come to the ICU to ask for guidance and advice about patient management. Furthermore, as we were pulmonologists in addition to intensivists, we provided pulmonary consultation services to patients admitted to the hospital. All physicians who worked in the hospital benefited from this model, as the in-house pulmonary/critical care medicine physician evaluated their patients with complex pulmonary issues promptly.

The benefits of this system also extended to physicians in the greater community, who would phone for an opinion about a complex pulmonary patient and receive prompt advice day or night from the in-house pulmonary/critical care physician.

Not surprisingly, the utility of this model extended well beyond hospital walls. Physicians in the community constantly shared feedback with the hospital about how much they valued having round-the-clock access to a pulmonologist/critical care physician. Physicians in outlying hospitals were the backbone of the referral system for WMC.

## THE CORPORATE TAKEOVER

In the latter part of 2019, the hospital was taken over by a large healthcare system. The intensivist model had been delivering this high standard of patient care for over a decade. By the time COVID-19 arrived in our community in February 2020 we enjoyed many benefits from being part of a larger healthcare system. We were able to maintain the required number of nurses at the bedside, enjoy a generous supply of personal protective equipment, and access the system's large infectious disease database. These resources were critical for enabling us to stay safe and provide the highest quality of patient care. Like all of us working in hospital settings, we endured shattering experiences as we fought through the pandemic.

Fast-forward to January 2022. Our team's first encounter with the hospital's new management came on the other side of the pandemic crisis, when we were asked to sit down with the Western Region administrators and discuss our bonus for the previous year. Our CMO and the hospital system's director of practice operations were also present. We were informed that we would not receive our full bonus due to us because we had failed to document in the electronic medical record the "Goals of Care" discussions with our patients or their family members/ medical powers of attorney.

Anyone who worked through COVID, who gave their all to the hardest year of their careers and endured unimaginable stress and trauma—indeed, who risked their lives—can likely identify with our shock and outrage. Making a good "first impression" was of little importance to the regional executives. Silence filled the room as we physicians looked at each other in disbelief. We left the meeting feeling deflated, angry, unappreciated, and in no small measure taken advantage of.

I worked with the Chief Medical Officer (CMO) to illustrate how the patient chart audit was erroneous and that we had actually done a much better job of documenting "Goals of Care" discussions. The hospital management eventually decided to pay us 75% of the bonus money available for distribution. To say the gesture was shortsighted would be an understatement. Not soon after that, the ICU medical director handed in her resignation. She had been working as a pulmonary and critical care medicine physician at that hospital for 11 years.

## THE PERILS OF CORPORATE CHANGES

A few weeks after that momentous meeting, the CEO of the hospital asked us to explore the possibility of using remote ICU coverage at our hospital. Under this model of ICU care, also called e-ICU or virtual ICU, a remote intensivist would replace the nighttime in-house intensivist. The remote intensivist would be available by phone and would use remote technology to evaluate the patient and decide on a plan of treatment. They would cover an additional 20 to 30 critically ill patients throughout the network of more than 30 hospitals.

I asked, "What will happen if the patient is deteriorating and an intensivist is clearly needed at the bedside?"

Their response was "The nurse will call the daytime intensivist."

This would be the person who had just completed a 12-hour shift in the ICU. The lead presenter, who had never been in our hospital or worked in our ICU, explained that in his experience, having to call back the day-shift intensivist was exceedingly rare.

I explained that I had worked in this ICU for six years before we created the current intensivist model, and I had been called in approximately 50% of the nights I was on call. The remote model clearly would not provide the quality of treatment our critical care patients deserved.

## PROBLEMS WITH REMOTE ICU CARE

Remote monitoring technology has been employed in ICUs since the late 1990s. The published literature on the effectiveness of e-ICU care over the last two decades has been inconsistent, with some studies showing mortality benefits and cost savings and other studies showing the opposite.

To be fair, a virtual ICU may be extremely useful in remote locations with little or no access to a critical care specialist. However, they add little value to a facility with a strong intensivist presence (which was the case at my hospital). A study in the *New England Journal of Medicine* of 66,000 patients admitted to 49 ICUs in the United States confirms this (Wallace et al. 2012).

Given the many advantages to our existing model, I felt e-ICU would be a poor choice for our hospital. Likewise, asking an intensivist to work 12 hours straight in the ICU and then be on call all night for the next 12 hours was both unsafe and unsustainable. In addition, this arrangement would no doubt cause dissatisfaction among the medical staff and be a recruitment disincentive to boot. Intensivists have the highest rate of burnout among all medical subspecialties. The reason we created the intensivist model at my hospital in 2009 was to minimize burnout and to improve patient care and recruitment.

By this stage, I was the only intensivist from our initial group of five who had not resigned. I shared my concerns with my hospital's leadership, but I had the sense that not much could be done to rectify the situation at this stage. I felt my input didn't really matter.

Soon, I was informed that despite our concerns, hospital management had decided to transition to e-ICU at night. When I tried to advocate for the retention of our successful ICU model, the Western Division CMO said, "All hospitals think they are unique. Your average daily census is only eight patients."

This response was an example of what I call the "spreadsheet approach" to healthcare. Spreadsheets are lazy. They reveal nothing about culture, passion, or communication and teamwork. Some days, a physician spends five hours with just one patient trying to save their life. This could never be captured on a spreadsheet.

I gave my written notice the next day.

## THE ROOT CAUSES OF THE PROBLEM

I understand the CEO's perspective. Due to the national shortage of pulmonary and critical care physicians, the hospital was experiencing great difficulty recruiting them. Under these circumstances, the next best option was to utilize virtual coverage for the ICU at night. But of course, the way in which the decision was made and communicated created an extremely negative physician experience with catastrophic consequences.

The real issue at the heart of this story is the misalignment of values and the failure of each party to find a common middle ground from which to maintain a complex, high-functioning unit. Maybe in the future better virtual ICU systems will prove to be equal to an in-person intensivist. However, at present, the peer-reviewed, published data does not support such an approach. Nor does my personal experience. Taking more time to understand each other and why we see things the way we do would have served all of us better.

This case study highlights a common collision of values in contemporary healthcare: cost containment/profitability versus doing what's best for patient care . . . *as articulated by those providing the care.* It is my hope that the insights shared in this story will prove valuable to CEOs charged with managing this delicate balance on a daily basis.

## THE MORAL OF THE STORY

The lesson here is intuitive. If you are a hospital CEO, or if you deal with healthcare leadership in some way, it is crucial that you recognize the importance of the physician as customer and the quality of service delivered. Failure to provide a high level of physician customer service will give rise to alienation and, ultimately, poor physician retention.

Patients, of course, benefit from doctors who are present, both literally and figuratively. And doctors who are not overextended are obviously going to provide better treatment. The quality of care remains high when the best physicians want to remain employed at their workplaces.

Take time to consider your primary customers' insights and wisdom. Reflect on ways you can integrate physicians' observations and analysis within your institution.

CHAPTER ELEVEN

# A NEW WAY TO RUN A HOSPITAL

HOW YOU SEE yourself and how you function within a hospital setting can sometimes be an obstacle to change.

If you give a low priority to a culture of excellent physician service throughout the organization, nothing will change. In contrast, if you view all healthcare providers within your organization as your most important customers and the key to better patient outcomes and economic success, then your organization will become dynamic and innovative. It will quickly distinguish itself from the competition.

I've observed that as a hospital system expands, responsibility for the physician experience and relationship-building moves down the corporate chain. This, in my opinion, is a strategic error. It sends a message that the CEO wants to have less involvement with physicians. CEOs who genuinely wish to improve the customer experience for the hospital's care providers will encourage an open-door policy and go out of their way to make themselves more available.

## ADMINISTRATIVE ROLES

Each person in an administrative role has the potential to contribute to the physician customer experience, either positively or negatively.

Most hospital CEOs are primarily focused on the vision, growth, and expansion of the hospital's services. Ensuring the hospital's financial survival is paramount. CEOs operating within a large healthcare system may delegate physician-related issues to a separate group of administrators who manage all the employed physicians within the corporation. By comparison, local hospital CEOs tend to actively seek out physician engagement and relationship-building, and rarely delegate this activity. In a well-functioning hospital, of course, the physician customer experience is central to the quality of care and the hospital's financial success, and the CEO strives to keep their focus on physician satisfaction and well-being.

Meanwhile, the traditional role of the CMO is that of a go-between for the medical staff and the administrative staff. That usually amounts to being the clinical quality control and behavior control officer for the medical staff. The CMO enforces the hospital's policies and guidelines and acts as an intermediary between the needs of the organization and the needs of the physicians. The person in this position has great potential to improve the physician customer experience. This is more likely to occur when the CEO and the CMO are fully aligned on the importance of cultivating a culture of customer service.

For example, one way the CMO can support the CEO would be to attend physician team meetings (for example, when ICU doctors get together to discuss issues) a couple of times a year and specifically focus on examples of poor physician customer experience/service within the organization and how to resolve the issues raised.

The chief of medical staff is a practicing physician elected by the medical staff to represent their issues to the hospital administration and thus is positioned to serve as the doctors' advocate. Yet this physician is usually a busy clinician who may or may not possess great leadership skills. The person in this role attends the hospital's monthly committee meetings and provides updates to the medical staff throughout the year. Tensions and difficulties are inherent to this job, as it is generally voluntary with no protected time away from clinical responsibilities and no financial reimbursement. And while members of the medical staff will commonly voice their concerns to this person, the chief of medical staff has no decision-making authority.

One way to improve this dynamic would be for the hospital CEO to hold a bimonthly meeting with the chief of medical staff to receive updates on feedback received from care providers. A better-informed CEO and a more-empowered chief of medical staff are integral to improving physician customer experience within the organization.

Middle management also plays a pivotal role in cultivating the physician customer experience. Hospital professionals such as practice managers and nursing unit managers are frequently the face of physician customer service in action. I still think frequently of Rita, a practice manager I used to work with. Rita made you feel as though she constantly had your back. She was supportive and helpful no matter what the issue was, which made my job so much more enjoyable. In addition, as medical director of the ICU, I worked closely with Jenea, the ICU nurse manager. Jenea was a great listener. I felt heard and understood and knew that my position would be accurately represented by the higher levels of the hospital administration.

The sum of such individual interactions with those in leadership is what creates the hospital's culture. Each professional's role simply provides the opportunity for engagement. The obstacle to transforming and maintaining a culture of physician service excellence is not the role, but rather the mindset and desire to do so.

## WHAT GETS IN THE WAY

Lee devotes a chapter to closing the gap between knowing and doing. He makes the case that most managers already know what they need to attain customer satisfaction in the services they can control. However, inertia seems to stop them from turning knowledge into action.

Lee outlines several traps managers commonly fall into that prevent them from closing the gap between knowledge and doing. These are worth summarizing here.

- "Expecting committees to transform the culture"
  Lee captures this mindset with the dictum "Attend a two-day training program and all will be well." Unless managers genuinely buy into, model, and require the new behavior, nothing will change.

- "Hiring a service excellence coordinator"
  These people have no line authority over employees and thus have little or no impact, Lee argues. Basically, if the

CEO pays attention to something, then the rest of the managers and employees will, too.

- "Thinking more knowledge will close the gap"
  The reality, Lee says, is that *doing* is what's missing, not more knowledge. Leadership requires action, "walking the talk," focusing on what's most important in the customer's experience, coaching others, and doing things that win the hearts of the customers.

- "Letting assessment substitute for action"
  Lee reminds us that feedback does not in itself result in action. If that were the case, simply showing your employee the report or the graph would transform attitudes and behavior.

- "Permitting managers to stall indefinitely with HOW questions"
  How long will it take?
  How much will it cost?
  How do we measure it?

Asking such questions, Lee points out, can be a favorite defense against taking action.

We learn the most effective ways to do things through trial and error, as highlighted by the world's most famous marketing/advertising slogan "Just do it." Action results through doing, not merely thinking, planning, listening, or talking.

If you are a competent and self-confident manager and want it badly enough, you will find a way. More knowledge will not lead to action if a manager is not deeply and intensely committed to it.

We do not need more administrators to change the culture within the hospital. As it stands, most hospitals are already administrator-heavy: between 1975 and 2010, the number of US physicians grew by 150% while the number of healthcare administrators increased by 3,200% (Chandrashekar and Jain 2019).

The major obstacle to culture change and improved physician customer service is not the organizational structure or the roles that already exist; it is mindset. Adopting a new perspective and growth mindset that prioritizes customer service and takes action to deliver on this is what can shift the tide.

## THE DIRECTION HOSPITALS NEED

Attitude and behavior change culture, and this must start with the CEO. In fact, physician customer service must become the CEO's daily obsession. This is the only way it will become an accepted and expected standard within the organization. It should not matter which manager or department a physician interacts with: if the culture has been transformed, a positive customer experience will be the norm, not the exception.

But what about hospitals that have been consumed by healthcare systems? If you are a CEO in this situation, you might wonder what changes are within your power to effect. It is important to recognize that the local CEO does not need permission from the corporate office to instill a culture of providing service excellence to its physicians. Quite the contrary, if physicians enjoy high levels of job satisfaction and have lower turnover rates and deliver better patient care, the hospital metrics will speak for themselves.

CEOs can't achieve this alone, however. For the process to work, communication from physicians is vital. Physicians have a responsibility to speak up and inform the hospital CEO about poor service if they want it to change. Venting to each other in the hospital corridors is not speaking up.

Eyal Press's *New York Times Magazine* article "The Moral Crisis of America's Doctors" (June 15, 2023) highlights the reluctance of many physicians to speak out against their employers from fear of being perceived as disruptive. Physicians so labeled are frequently subject to sanctions and may even lose their jobs. Thus, they complain to their colleagues but don't want to rock the boat with the hospital administration. The psychological effect and sequence of events is predictable. Symptoms of burnout emerge, and doctors tend to disengage from their work. Ultimately, they resign from the hospital, and so begins the cycle of recruitment yet again.

A hospital CEO who is serious about providing a positive physician experience will want to know about poor service and find ways to improve it. The culture should be such that this form of feedback is welcomed, and no physician would be penalized for communicating concerns.

CEOs and physicians will benefit from working together to transform hospital culture. Try to seek out examples of poor physician customer experience and collaboratively explore ways to improve it. Make this a priority throughout all hospital managerial departments, and you are likely to see your institution flourish.

## INVESTING IN CHANGE

Money and time could also be viewed as obstacles to improving the physician customer experience. It is true that modeling a behavior and changing the culture of a hospital and its system take time, but nothing like the time it takes to recruit a new physician.

Regarding money, I can think of no better return on investment than improving physician customer experience throughout a hospital system.

## PROFIT AS AN OBSTACLE?

Despite the profitability of some US hospitals, an increasing number find themselves in dire financial straits. Between 53% and 68% of the nation's hospitals were expected to end 2022 with their operations in the red, compared to 34% reported for 2019 (Muoio 2022).

But profitability brings its own risks. Inertia induced by a hospital's current profitability could become an obstacle to improving physician customer service.

This is not as rare a problem as you might think. For instance, while 57% of US hospitals are nonprofit, many of them are extremely profitable.

Hospitals that wish to maintain their profitability—or forestall further losses—may hesitate to invest in improvements to their customer service culture. However, worsening physician retention presents a bigger and more important barrier to a hospital's sustained growth and bottom line. Many currently profitable hospitals may not stay that way for long if they cannot retain their physicians. Not only will they have to cover the cost of recruitment per physician, but they will also endure lower productivity and the loss of patient care revenue. And any significant increase in labor costs in the coming years may be enough to force more hospitals to close.

## A FINAL NOTE

I certainly don't have to tell you that managing a hospital or a healthcare system is complex and challenging. The healthcare space is one of the most regulated industries in the country and is currently experiencing unprecedented change. Moreover, the current staffing crisis within the industry has created new opportunities and obstacles for CEOs and healthcare providers alike. The CEO's balancing act to ensure both positive financial performance and a workplace culture that generates high levels of physician job satisfaction is no small challenge. And those of you walking that tightrope deserve respect and support as your perspective and depth of understanding evolve.

It is my hope that this book has taken you on a unique journey, one that shares the perspective of the physician as the organization's primary customer. I have aimed to equip you with the tools necessary to build an exemplary customer experience and recruit and retain high-caliber physicians while maintaining high profitability.

Listen to your physicians. Give thought to their perspectives. Provide them with the consideration and resources they require.

Such a change in orientation is critical within the current US healthcare system. I have no doubt that CEOs and hospitals that make physician customer experience a priority will enjoy a significant financial return on their investment. All hospitals aspire to provide excellent patient care. Providing exceptional customer service to your employed physicians is the surest way to achieve this goal.

# ABOUT THE AUTHOR

**MARK J. MC GINLEY, MD,** was born in Drogheda, Ireland, and grew up in Armagh, Northern Ireland. His family immigrated to South Africa in 1976, where he completed his high school years and university education. He has a Bachelor of Commerce degree from the University of Natal majoring in Psychology and Business Administration. He has a medical degree from the University of Cape Town medical school. Mark immigrated to the United States in 1992 and has been practicing as a specialist in pulmonary medicine and critical care medicine since 1998.

Dr. Mc Ginley has extensive experience working with hospital administrators to build programs that benefit both physicians and patients. He created the intensivist program at Wyoming Medical Center in 2009 and served as the medical director for six years. He also established the NERD Wellness Center at WMC in 2016 and served as its first medical director.

Mark currently lives in Denver, Colorado, with his wife and enjoys an active lifestyle. He divides his time between direct patient care, speaking, and consulting on how to improve the customer experience in healthcare.

*Critical Relief* is his first book.

To inquire about speaking or consulting engagements, visit CriticalRelief.com.

# REFERENCES

"AAMC Report Reinforces Mounting Physician Shortage." AAMC.org. June 11, 2021. https://www.aamc.org/news/press-releases/aamc-report-reinforces-mounting-physician-shortage.

Anumula, N., and P. C. Sanelli. "Meaningful Use." National Library of Medicine. NIH.gov. *American Journal of Neuroradiology*. September 2012. https://pubmed.ncbi.nlm.nih.gov/22790244/.

Berg, Sara. "How much physician burnout is costing your organization." American Medical Association. October 11, 2018. https://www.ama-assn.org/practice-management/physician-health/how-much-physician-burnout-costing-your-organization.

Chandrashekar, Pooja, and Sachin H. Jain. "Understanding and Fixing the Growing Divide Between Physicians and Healthcare Administrators." PDF. March/April 2019. https://drive.google.com/file/d/1e51TKz4YZOTqpElMHvE3D2eYNiaM9Zeq/view.

Collier, Roger. "Electronic health records contributing to physician burnout." National Library of Medicine. NIH.gov. *Canadian Medical Association Journal*. November 13, 2017. https://www.ncbi.nlm.nih.gov/pmc/articles/PMC5687935/.

"Consumer Assessment of Healthcare Providers and Systems (CAHPS)." Centers for Medicare & Medicaid Services. CMS.gov. Last modified April 21, 2024. https://www.cms.gov/data-research/research/consumer-assessment-healthcare-providers-systems.

Densen, Peter. "Challenges and Opportunities Facing Medical Education." National Library of Medicine. NIH.gov. *Transactions of the American Clinical and Climatological Association*. 2011. https://www.ncbi.nlm.nih.gov/pmc/articles/PMC3116346/.

Diaz, Naomi. "96% of US hospitals have EHRs, but barriers remain to interoperability, ONC says." BeckersHospitalReview.com. March 7, 2023. https://www.beckershospitalreview.com/ehrs/96-of-us-hospitals-have-ehrs-but-barriers-remain-to-interoperability-onc-says.html.

DiMatteo, M.R. et al. "Physicians' characteristics influence patients' adherence to medical treatments: results from the Medical Outcomes Study." National Library of Medicine. NIH.gov. *Health Psychology*. March 1993. https://pubmed.ncbi.nlm.nih.gov/8500445/.

Firth-Cozens, J., and J. Greenhalgh. "Doctor's perceptions of the links between stress and lowered clinical care." National Library of Medicine. NIH.gov. *Social Science & Medicine*. April 1997. https://pubmed.ncbi.nlm.nih.gov/9089922/.

Frich, Jan C. et al. "Leadership development programs for physicians: a systematic review." National Library of Medicine. NIH.gov. *Journal of General Internal Medicine*. December 20, 2014. https://pubmed.ncbi.nlm.nih.gov/25527339/.

"Great Expectations: Making Hybrid Work *Work*." Work Trend Index Annual Report. Microsoft.com. March 16, 2022. https://www.microsoft.com/en-us/worklab/work-trend-index/great-expectations-making-hybrid-work-work.

Gui, Xinning et al. "Physician champions' perspectives and practices on electronic health records implementation: challenges and strategies." National Library of Medicine. NIH.gov. JAMIA Open. January 7, 2020. https://pubmed.ncbi.nlm.nih.gov/32607488/.

Gunja, Munira Z., Evan D. Gumas, and Reginald D. Williams II. "U.S. Health Care from a Global Perspective, 2022: Accelerating Spending, Worsening Outcomes." The Commonwealth Fund. CommonwealthFund.org. January 2023. https://www.commonwealthfund.org/publications/issue-briefs/2023/jan/us-health-care-global-perspective-2022.

Hartzband, Pamela, and Jerome Groopman. "Physician Burnout, Interrupted." *The New England Journal of Medicine*. May 1, 2020. https://www.nejm.org/doi/full/10.1056/NEJMp2003149.

Henderson, Wendy et al. "A New Approach to New Physician Orientation: Six Key Components." *Family Practice Management*. AAFP.org. 2019. https://www.aafp.org/pubs/fpm/issues/2019/0700/p24.html.

Humphrey-Murto, Susan et al. "Training physicians and residents for the use of Electronic Health Records—A comparative case study between two hospitals." *Medical Education*. April 2023. https://pubmed.ncbi.nlm.nih.gov/36181382/.

Kohn, Linda T., Janet M. Corrigan, and Molla S. Donaldson, editors. "To Err is Human: Building a Safer Health System." National Library of Medicine. NIH.gov. Institute of Medicine (US) Committee on Quality of Health Care in America. PubMed. 2000. https://pubmed.ncbi.nlm.nih.gov/25077248/.

Lee, Fred. 2004. *If Disney Ran Your Hospital: 9½ Things You Would Do Differently*. Second River Healthcare.

Lubman, Dan, Kate Hall, and Tanya Gibbie. "Motivational interviewing techniques: Facilitating behaviour change in the general practice setting." *Australian Family Physician*. RACGP .org.au. September 2012. https://www.racgp.org.au/afp/2012/september/motivational-interviewing-techniques.

Madden, Blake. "Diving into Physician Corporatization: The Latest Numbers on Physician Employment." Hospitalogy.com. April 18, 2024. https://hospitalogy.com/articles/2024–04-18/corporatization-physician-employment/

Maslach Burnout Inventory—Human Services Survey (MBI-HSS) for Medical Personnel. https://nam.edu/valid-reliable-survey-instruments-measure-burnout-well-work-related-dimensions.

Mazurenko, Olena, Dina Marie Zemke, and Noelle Lefforge. "Who Is a Hospital's 'Customer'?" National Library of Medicine. NIH.gov. *Journal of Healthcare Management*. September/October 2016. https://pubmed.ncbi.nlm.nih.gov/28319969/.

"Millennial Physicians: High in Numbers, Hard to Recruit—Here's What You Need to Know." *The Journal of Urgent Care Medicine*. JUCM.com. October 28, 2019. https://www.jucm.com/millennial-physicians-high-in-numbers-hard-to-recruit-heres-what-you-need-to-know.

Mind Garden. MindGarden.com. https://www.mindga

Muoio, Dave. " 'Unsustainable' losses are forcing hospitals to make 'heart-wrenching' cuts and closures, leaders warn." FierceHealthcare.com. September 16, 2022. www.fiercehealthcare.com/providers/unsustainable-losses-are-forcing-hospitals-make-heart-wrenching-cuts-and-closures-leaders.

Nguyen, Kim-Huong et al. "Economic evaluation and analyses of hospital-based electronic medical records (EMRs): a scoping review of international literature." *npj Digital Medicine*. March 8, 2022. https://www.nature.com/articles/s41746–022-00565–1.

"Physician burnout rate spikes to new height." American Medical Association. September 15, 2022. https://www.ama-assn.org/press-center/press-releases/physician-burnout-rate-spikes-new-height.

Press, Eyal. "The Moral Crisis of America's Doctors." *New York Times Magazine*. June 15, 2023. https://www.nytimes.com/2023/06/15/magazine/doctors-moral-crises.html.

"Understanding the Physician Passive Jobseeker." *New England Journal of Medicine*. NEJMCareerCenter.org. https://www.nejmcareercenter.org/minisites/rpt/understanding-the-physician-passive-jobseeker-/.

Wallace, David J. et al. "Nighttime Intensivist Staffing and Mortality among Critically Ill Patients." *New England Journal of Medicine*. May 31, 2012. https://www.nejm.org/doi/full/10.1056/NEJMsa1201918.

# ACKNOWLEDGMENTS

THIS BOOK WOULD not have come to publication were it not for the magnificent team at Modern Wisdom Press. I wish to thank the cofounders, Catherine Gregory and Nathan Joblin, who are also published authors. Catherine, your process for supporting me in getting clear on my message and my audience was both novel and inspiring. Nathan, you took the stress out of the technical aspects of production. I also wish to thank the editors, Gabrielle Idlet, Felicia Lee, and Julie Willson. I am extremely grateful for your guidance and editorial refinements.

I would like to thank all those who agreed to interview with me. In particular, Wendy Castaldo (physician recruiter at Tenet Healthcare), Dr. Robert Colbert (retired pulmonary and critical care physician), Paul Lobdell (clinical pharmacist at Banner Wyoming Medical Center), Dr. Richard Friedland (CEO of Netcare Group South Africa) and Matt Dammeyer, PhD (CEO of Memorial Hospital of Converse County). Sharing your insights and suggestions helped me to clarify my message.

To my wife, Andie, thank you for your relentless support and encouragement. This book took longer to complete than I thought it would, and no one knows that better than you. To my three children, Ciara, Claire, and John, you have heard me discussing this book for the better part of two years. We have had many laughs and created great memories debating customer service (or lack thereof) over the years on our travels. I doubt that will ever change. I look forward to continuing to learn from you.

Last but by no means least, I wish to thank my father, Joe Mc Ginley, for a lifetime of love and support. You have always been my greatest fan. An education in commerce and medicine would not have been possible without your support. I learned the art of good communication from observing you. I hope that is evident in my current writings. Thanks, Dad.

# ABOUT MODERN WISDOM PRESS

FOUNDED BY Catherine Gregory and Nathan Joblin in 2019, Modern Wisdom Press is dedicated to elevating conscious voices by empowering visionary leaders and subject matter experts to find clarity, ease, and joy in writing and publishing their transformational nonfiction books.

Our values and core principles are rooted in conscious leadership, which begins with self-awareness and intentionality, awakening more fulfillment and purpose in your life and those you lead. We support aspiring authors who are here to make a positive impact, with the ripple effect benefiting not only their readers, but also their families, communities, and beyond.

modern wisdom
PRESS